AQUARIUM FILTRATION

RICHARD F. STRATTON

I t wasn't that long ago that the equipment used for filtering home aquaria was relatively primitive, concentrating as it did on the purely cosmetic aspects of aquarium management. Gradually, however, the aquarium hobby became more aware of biological processes that play a very important part in determining whether an aquarium—big or little, freshwater or saltwater, featuring coldwater or truly tropical animals—-will be successful or not. But the situation has changed. Today the problem facing an aquarist new to the ways of things fishy is not so much a case of finding out whether it's possible to keep the water in a tank from turning murky as it is a case of deciding which of the many filtration options—or combination of options—is the one that best suits your pocketbook, your fishes' needs, your temperament and your available space situation.

That's what this publication will try to do for you: to present enough information about the ways different filtration systems operate and their comparative advantages and disadvantages to let you make up your own mind about what will do the best job for you. But don't forget that books and magazines are not the only sources of information open to you. You should also be able to learn plenty from experienced hobbyists and from tropical fish livestock and equipment dealers as well, all of whom have already served their apprenticeships in the hobby and have potentially valuable information to pass along.

What are Quarterlies?

Books, the usual way information of this sort is transmitted, can be too slow. Sometimes by the time a book is written and published, the material contained therein is a year or two old...and no new material has been added during that time. Only a book in a magazine form can bring breaking stories and current information. A magazine is streamlined in production, so we have adopted certain magazine publishing techniques in the creation of this Aquarium Quarterly. Magazines also can be much cheaper than books because they are supported by advertising. To combine these assets into a great publication, we are issuing this Quarterly in both magazine and book format at different prices.

yearBOOKS,INC.

Dr. Herbert R. Axelrod,
Founder & Chairman

Glen S. Axelrod
President & Chief Executive Officer

Gary Hersch
Executive Vice President

Barry Duke
Chief Operating Officer

Neal Pronek
Managing Editor

yearBOOKS are all photo composed, color separated and designed on Scitex equipment in Neptune, N.J. with the following staff:

DIGITAL PRE-PRESS
Patricia Northrup
Supervisor

Robert Onyrscuk
Jose Reyes

COMPUTER ART
Patti Escabi
Candida Moreira
Joanne Muzyka
Francine S. Shulman

ADVERTISING SALES
Nancy S. Rivadeneira
Advertising Sales Director

Cheryl J. Blyth
Advertising Account Manager

Amy Manning
Advertising Director

Frances Wrona
Advertising Coordinator

©yearBOOKS, Inc.
1 TFH Plaza
Neptune, N.J. 07753
Completely manufactured in
Neptune, N.J.
USA

Cover design by Sherise Buhagiar

CONTENTS

FILTRATION:
THE HEART OF THE AQUARIUM

Filtration is the heart of any aquarium system because water is the lifeblood of the aquarium, having an immediate direct effect on everything that lives in it. Since water is so important, it is up to us to keep it in good shape. One of the ways that we do that is through the use of filtration.

Usually when we think of filtration, we think of simply filtering debris out of the water. But filtration is much more complex than that. However, it is our intent to keep everything as simple as possible. Why make things any more complicated than is absolutely required? Besides, it is useful to separate out the simple things and deal with them, leaving aside complicating factors that don't immediately concern us. That is what we do in mathematics, classical physics, and a number of other scientific disciplines.

As our first step in simplifying, let us divide all filtration into two simple categories: mechanical and biological. For our purposes, mechanical filtration is filtration that has as its major purpose the removal of debris from the water. That is all that the pioneering tropical fish hobbyists wanted, good and clean water so that they could see their beautiful charges all the better. It was noted, though, that the older aquaria seemed to do better than the new aquaria. That is, aquaria that had been up and running for several months, or even years, did better than brand new and shiny tanks that were set up.

Because the fishes and other animals lived better and seemed healthier in the older aquaria, it was deduced that there was something special about the water. Old water was greatly valued. It is amusing to read some of the

Usually a tank that looks clean is clean, at least in the sense that it does not have a lot of particulate matter suspended in the water—but keeping a tank free of suspended matter is only a part of the job that an aquarium filter has to perform.

The quality of the water in a marine aquarium makes itself felt even more swiftly than in a freshwater aquarium, because marine animals, marine invertebrates especially, are in general more sensitive to polluting elements. Photo by U. Erich Friese.

old aquarium books now and note their emphasis on well aged water. But these pioneers were not entirely off the track. They found that they were more successful if they started out a new aquarium by filling it, at least part way, with prized water taken from some long-successful aquarium. Although the more astute hobbyists suspected that there was some biological process going on, others simply accepted that there was something "magical" about old aquarium water.

Now we know that there certainly was a biological process going on. What was happening was that beneficial bacteria had colonized the walls, the ornaments, the plants, and the gravel of the old aquarium. These bacteria (which we will cover in more detail later) broke down nitrogen waste products given off by the fishes and by excess food. These products were broken down into simpler and less toxic byproducts. An established aquarium had millions of these bacteria, and they could easily process metabolic products given off by the fishes. There was

nothing magical about the water after all, but the actions of the bacteria can seem magical even now.

To understand how the bacteria work and just what they do, it is useful to discuss the nitrogen cycle. It is discussed in nearly every aquarium book (modern ones, that is) almost to the point of boredom and may seem pedantic and dull, but it is not difficult to follow. Just give me five minutes of your time here and you will easily understand some of the important chemical changes that go on in your aquarium.

THE NITROGEN CYCLE

The Earth itself is a closed system with respect to materials. Water, carbon, nitrogen, phosphorus, and the other building materials of living tissues are cycled perpetually through organisms to the environment and back again, also through organisms. For some minerals the cycles are closed, meaning that virtually all of the molecules are kept in constant circulation. For others the cycles are very "leaky," large quantities of the minerals being temporarily lost from circulation through deposition in deep sea sediments, where they are unavailable until some future period of mountain building

Aquarists years ago did not have the many advantages available to today's hobbyists in terms of equipment and knowledge, but they still were able to keep and breed many different fish species successfully. Set up in the 1950s, this aquarium and its decor look quaint today but were in step with the times. Photo by Laurence E. Perkins.

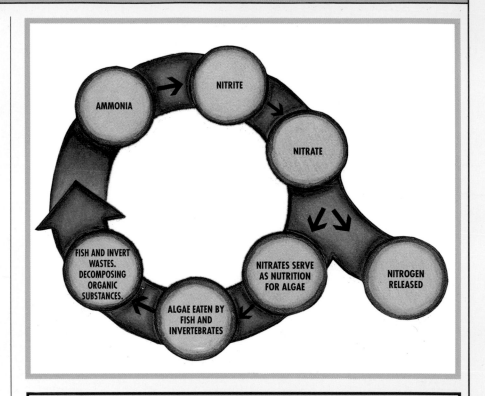

A depiction of the nitrogen cycle, showing that the ammonia compounds produced as a result of decay and animal metabolism can be rendered progressively less toxic by beneficial bacteria. Drawing by John Quinn.

elevates those sediments above sea level and initiates a new cycle of weathering. The carbon and nitrogen atoms of which we are composed today are the same atoms that were in dinosaurs, insects, and trees in the Mesozoic era.

Each of the biogeochemical cycles has its own distinctive pathways and rates of flow. Examples are the cycles of carbon and nitrogen. In both cycles, general circulation occurs primarily in the gaseous phase in the atmosphere. Cycling is fast through living organisms because no individual, even of the longest-lived species, lives very long (in geological terms), and death and decomposition rapidly release the minerals that are taken up again by other organisms. It is when

molecules escape from the terrestrial ecosystem into the ocean that they tend to be lost for long periods of time.

In the aquarium, we are dealing with a closed system of significantly smaller dimensions than the entire planet. For that reason, among others, we are primarily concerned about the nitrogen cycle, and the "catabolic" aspect at that. That is the part of the cycle in which complex nitrogen-bearing organic compounds are sequentially broken down into simpler substances. But let us go through the entire cycle.

Excretion from the animals and excess food results in urine, feces, and peptides and amino acids. All of these substances degrade into ammonia (NH_3), which is quite toxic to fishes. That is why the pioneering hobbyists all had trouble with freshly set up new tanks, with new filters operating. They didn't know what was happening, but they had a name for it: new tank syndrome. What was happening was that there was not yet a colony of bacteria established for breaking down the ammonia.

The chemical formula for ammonia, NH_3, means that each molecule of ammonia has one atom of nitrogen and three of hydrogen. Nitrifying bacteria break the ammonia down into nitrite (NO_3). The chemical formula in this case means that each molecule of nitrite has one atom of nitrogen and three of oxygen. Nitrite is still toxic to fishes, but other species of nitrifying bacteria break this compound down into nitrate (NO_2). The loss of a single atom of oxygen

makes a big difference in the toxicity of the compound, as nitrate is tolerated quite well by most fishes. A problem is that it can be tough on some marine invertebrates, and nitrate is difficult to get out of the aquarium. That is why most freshwater hobbyists make regular partial water changes: to diminish the nitrate by dilution. However, filtration has made many strides throughout the years, and at least partial elimination of nitrate is now possible.

Part of the nitrate is taken up by algae and by plants. In fact, this is one of the solutions to the problem of nitrate in the natural aquarium systems, which we will discuss later. In any case, this is the completion of the nitrogen cycle as the nitrate is taken up by plants (or algae) for use in their tissues. The cycle would begin once again with fish eating the plants and

discharging metabolic byproducts into the water. In the aquarium, the cycle is not confined to the tank, as hobbyists are not desirous of having fish that eat the plants. So food is introduced from outside the tank. (And, of course, many aquarists don't keep live plants, as plastic ones can be more practical. Also, some fish, such as the very popular cichlids, can be quite tough on plants.)

TEST KITS

Good aquarium practices always involve managing the nitrogen process by not overfeeding the fishes to the point that food is left uneaten. Other considerations are selections of mechanical and biological filters. Mechanical filters should have their filtering elements changed frequently enough that the organic matter collected is not allowed to decompose. It

An accumulation of nitrates in the aquarium water is especially dangerous to invertebrates such as these sponges, *Verongula rigida*. Photo by U. Erich Friese.

In a freshwater aquarium heavily stocked with healthy plants, the nitrate content of the water could be somewhat reduced because of the plants' capacity for taking up some of the nitrates—but it would be unwise to rely on plants alone to reduce an aquarium's nitrate content. Photo by M-P and C. Piednoir, Aqua Press.

Caulerpa verticillata, one of the algae that serve to reduce nitrate levels in marine aquaria if provided with proper lighting. Photo by U. Erich Friese.

must be remembered that as long as the organic matter is in the filter, it is still part of the system.

Whatever biological filters are selected, it will take time for the desired bacteria to colonize whatever element is in the filter, whether it is sand, plastic balls, or ceramic noodles (or something else!). One way to start out a new tank is to set everything up with only a few small fishes so that the ammonia does not build up rapidly. Test kits will let you know when the bacterial colony is large enough to do the job.

The fact is that test kits have been a real boon to tropical fish hobbyists, as you can't tell whether the water is good for the fishes by just looking at it. There are kits for testing the level of ammonia, nitrite, and nitrate, not to mention kits for testing pH, oxygen levels, and redox potential, to

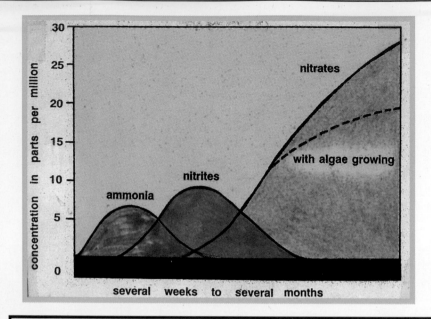

Graphic representation of the peaking and leveling of nitrite and nitrate levels in a newly set up aquarium. Drawing by John Quinn.

mention only a few. The most essential kits are those for testing ammonia, nitrite, and nitrate.

There is a characteristic pattern that is followed in the new tank. The ammonia level begins to build and

build. It finally peaks and then falls precipitously. This is a sign that the desired bacterial colony has become established. A different species of bacteria will process the nitrite, so a similar profile can be graphed for the nitrite level. It will build shortly after the ammonia level peaks, and then it, too, will fall off dramatically. At this time, it is safe to add more fishes. It is worth noting here that the bacterial colonies would not have developed without some fish life being present or some fish food being put into the tank to produce the ammonia upon which the bacteria feed. Some hobbyists simply feed the filter ammonia, but this is risky for the inexperienced, as it is difficult to provide just the right amount of ammonia at the proper times.

Experienced hobbyists will frequently utilize the test

Test kits of many types are available to measure a number of different qualities of aquarium water, both fresh and salt.

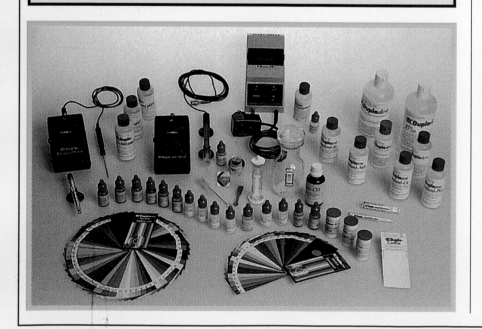

kits less than neophytes, for they have learned to observe their livestock and to practice good aquarium habits. In other words, everything becomes second nature with them; however, they got that way from using test kits to tell them what was happening in their water.

FRESHWATER VS. MARINE

It always seems as though marine hobbyists have so much more equipment than freshwater hobbyists that what they do must be different. The fact is that many of the same filtration systems are utilized in both aquarium types. It is just that marine hobbyists have two important reasons to be more persnickety about their water. The first is that their animals have evolved in a very stable environment, and thus they don't have the mechanisms for coping with change that the freshwater organisms have, so the water has to be kept pretty close to perfect. This is especially true in minireef aquaria, in which the emphasis is on invertebrates. It is only natural that such systems would become so popular. After all, some of the most impressive sea life is of the invertebrate type. Terrestrial invertebrates are nearly as numerous, but they have had to adapt to the pull of gravity by becoming small, and they are therefore less obvious.

The second reason that marine hobbyists have so

The invertebrates that inhabit minireef tanks demand stability of their environment and can easily be harmed by abrupt changes in water chemistry and temperature. Photo by Glen S. Axelrod.

much equipment is that water is more of a valuable commodity in the marine hobby. Synthetic salts have been a real boon to the hobby, but they still cost money, and it is one of the chores of the marine hobby to mix up new batches of water for the necessary regular partial water changes. It is no wonder that one of the goals in the marine hobby is to work toward a time that partial water changes are reduced or eliminated completely—a doubtful goal but a worthy one.

Hence marine hobbyists may utilize the same types of mechanical and biological filters as freshwater hobbyists, but a lot of redundancy may be built in. For example, a marine tank may have a trickle filter, a fluidized bed filter, and an undergravel filter—all examples of biological filtration. You can be sure that there will be plenty of mechanical filtration, too.

One of the beneficial byproducts of filtration is circulation of the aquarium water, necessary for many of the invertebrates in a marine tank. Photo by U. Erich Friese.

The idea is to keep the water in near-perfect condition and to keep it in that condition for longer periods of time. That is for the sake of the animals and for the conservation of the water.

About the only exclusively marine device is the protein skimmer. We will talk more about it later. It is sufficient now to say that it is a device for getting rid of organic compounds and is technically a chemical filter—although some may have difficulty with that concept—because it gets rid of the unwanted amino acids and peptides by foaming them out into a collection cup. It would be desirable to get rid of organics in fresh water, too, but fresh water is not sufficiently dense to provide the type of foaming action that is needed for good protein skimming.

The ozonizer, used for killing bacteria and parasites, is another device that is seldom seen on a freshwater aquarium. The ozone gas produced by the ozone generator will also oxidize organic matter from the water and can eliminate the yellowish tint that sometimes occurs in marine tanks. An ozone generator will work on a freshwater tank, but it is seldom used, because it is difficult to

A wet/dry filter coupled with a protein skimmer in use on a large marine aquarium at a commercial establishment. Photo by U. Erich Friese.

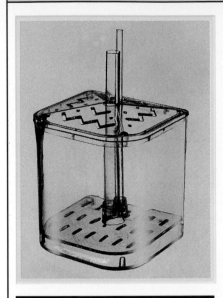

An older design among inside box, or corner, filters. They're not very hi-tech, but box filters still have important applications.

justify the cost when it is so easy to simply do regular partial water changes.

MECHANICAL AND BIOLOGICAL FILTERS

Very simply, all aquarium filtration falls into these two categories, but they don't do so neatly. That is, they don't always do so. Those initial aquarium pioneers that I spoke of earlier were astute enough to notice that the simple inside box filter seemed to be more effective when it had been run for a long time. This seemed to be counter to recommended practice, for it was (and still is) recommended that mechanical filters be changed on a regular basis. In this case, though, no biological filter had been set up deliberately, so the box filters performed the biological function once they had built up a sufficient colony of bacteria capable of breaking down ammonia and nitrite.

In a similar vein, the undergravel filter is both a biological filter and a mechanical filter. More properly, the undergravel filter is only a mechanical filter until the bacterial colony builds up. Then it begins to function biologically. In any case, it resists categorization as being purely either mechanical or biological, since it performs both functions, but it's generally classed as being much more biological than mechanical.

Many aquarists prefer to categorize filters into still more types, including chemical filtration. I will explain chemical filtration later. For now, just think of it as mechanical filtration at the molecular level. The point here is to keep things as simple as possible.

An excellent example of the need for both mechanical and biological filtration is the reverse-flow undergravel filter. This was an excellent improvement on that old workhorse, the undergravel filter. The idea is to keep the particulate matter separate from the biological filter. What happens is that the undergravel filter is supplied water by a canister filter. The canister filter provides prefiltered water underneath the filter plate. That is why the filter is called the reverse-flow undergravel filter. The gravel is still the home for the bacteria colony, but it does not become clogged with debris from particulate matter—or at least it takes a lot longer to become clogged. The theory was always that the bacteria would break down such debris, but the reality was that such particulate matter would get ahead of the bacteria and would form blockages so that channeling would occur, with more water being passed through certain parts of the gravel than

The arrows show the direction of water flow in this representation of how an undergravel filter works. Water pumped from the powerhead at the tip of the filter's riser tube creates a partial vacuum under the filter plate, causing water to flow downward through the gravel or other substance covering the plate. Drawing by John Quinn.

others. This situation not only leads to less efficient filtration but also can create dead spots, areas to which oxygen is not supplied. This gives anaerobic bacteria a chance to gain a foothold, and the trouble with them is that they can produce toxic gases. All of this is avoided with separate mechanical filtration. That is not to say that the undergravel filter can't be operated as originally intended, but a lot of gravel-stirring and vacuuming is needed to keep it operating properly.

Mechanical filtration can seem deceptively simple. It keeps the water polished and clear of debris, and all the hobbyist needs to do is to remember to change the elements on a regular basis. They can range from something as simple as an air-driven inside box filter with a little activated carbon and filter floss inside to an outside canister filter. The advantage of the latter is that it runs the water through the container (the canister) under pressure, and it is easier to disconnect and change the entrails of the filter without having any discharge get into the water. So popular have these units become that some have been designed for biological filtration, too. This is accomplished by providing compartments with different types of material for bacteria to colonize. Such units normally have a mechanical filter in the beginning of the flow, with the elements for bacterial colonization confined to other compartments. A measure of the popularity of these units is that it is not unusual to have one unit for mechanical filtration and one for biological.

Even though things get fuzzed a little when we try to categorize filters into either mechanical or biological classifications, it is useful to do so, as we can look at a setup and be sure in our minds that we have provided both these types of filters—even if they are in the same unit!

THE TRUE RULERS

Now for a word on behalf of bacteria. We are so used to thinking of bacteria as disease causers that we sometimes fail to remember that most species of bacteria do the work of the world. That is, life would be impossible for us "higher" animals if it were not for the work of bacteria breaking down compounds and building others that are important to us. Isaac Asimov referred to them as the true rulers because they were around for billions of years before other life, and they are equally likely to be around long after we have gone. They can live at greater extremes of the environment than we can, from hot sulfur springs to the cold Arctic (even if their life activity is much suppressed). The fact is that we couldn't live without bacteria, as they live symbiotically in our bodies and perform many functions, such as breaking down and producing compounds for us. The point is that we need to think of bacteria for the good they do for us, as well as the harm that is caused by the relatively few (as compared

> A canister filter operating on a freshwater aquarium. Water is drawn through the submerged wand, pumped through the canister and then returned through the spray bar. Drawing by John Quinn.

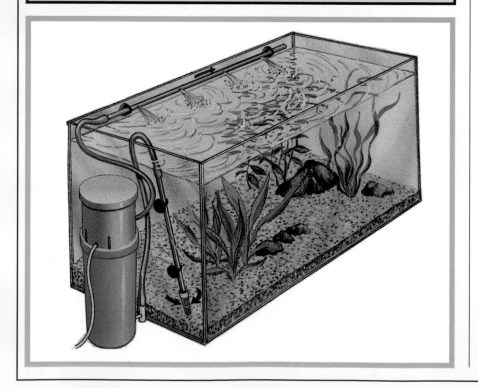

to the entire population) pathogenic types. Bacteria are the most ancient living form known, and they are quite successful in modern times, too. Although invisible to our eyes, they outnumber all other organisms in both number and bulk. They are now classified by scientists into their own kingdom of Prokaryotae (formerly Monera).

In the aquarium, we are primarily concerned with nitrifying bacteria that break down the nitrogen compounds. Such bacteria are the ones that change ammonia to nitrite and nitrite to nitrate. We are also interested in denitrifying bacteria; however, these bacteria work best in the absence of oxygen and are capable of expelling toxic gases. For that reason, they are utilized with care in special circumstances and devices. They are the bacteria that are capable of processing nitrate. And, of course, we should not forget decay bacteria, which break down food, feces, and other organic products into ammonia. There is a classification system for bacteria, and there are many phyla, families, and species, but it is fortunately not necessary for us to know exactly which species are at work for us.

In the aquarium, it is the nitrifying bacteria that we make the most use of in our various filters. It is worth noting, then, that such bacteria utilize oxygen in their work; most commercial filters make provision for this fact, as we will see.

Activated carbon can be one of the aquarist's most useful tools in providing chemical filtration. The sealable pouch is being used here to help reduce absorption by the carbon of airborne impurities.

CHEMICAL FILTRATION

Okay, in the interest of simplicity, I have been holding out on you. I said to simply consider chemical filtration as mechanical filtration at the molecular level. It is a little more complicated than that, but we will still keep it simple. Think of mechanical filtration as removing from the water debris that is in suspension and not dissolved. Removing dissolved gases, organics, and other substances is chemical filtration. This is done by the use of different grades of carbon, by ion exchange resins, and by water fractionators (protein skimmers).

There are three types of chemical filtration: absorption, ion-exchange, and adsorption. All three processes take place to some extent in most chemical filters, but let's take a close look at the processes themselves.

Absorption: Think of absorption as molecular sieving. This takes place in an activated carbon that has lots of surface area, and most of the area is inside the individual particles. There are so many tiny tunnels that run in so many different directions that the surface area of a single particle of carbon can be unbelievably great. Molecules in this case simply become trapped in the tiny little tunnels.

Adsorption: Think of this process as one in which a charge of some sort is involved. Thus, certain carbons attract organic molecules based on weak attractive charges (*Van der Waals forces*). This can also occur in a water-to-gas interface, and that is why a protein skimmer is technically a chemical filter. Complex organic molecules are polar on one end so that the end is attracted to water

A protein skimmer (the collection cup is visible above the water level at right in tank) at work in a tank holding a quantity of live rock. Photo by U. Erich Friese at JEM Aquatics.

to make up for the captured ionized molecule. Ion-exchange resins are rarely used in aquaria, but they are often used for softening water. Sometimes the resins are a component of an activated carbon mix used for aquarium filtration.

The reader can easily see why I tended to stay clear of chemical filtration, as even briefly touching upon it can be confusing. But then, nothing, it seems, is as simple as it seems. My point is that we can learn more by simplifying whenever possible. In any case, most filtration systems will include a chemical component someplace in them. And it is something to consider when you are putting together a filter system for your tank.

With some basis now of the purposes of filtration, let us take a look at some of the types of filters and how they perform their job in different ways.

and is called hydrophilic ("water loving"). The other end of the molecule is the "water hating" or hydrophobic end. These surface-active molecules are attracted to the water-gas surface of bubbles. Organic molecules adsorbed onto the surface of a bubble of air create a layer around it and form a foam. When the bubbles leave the water in the collection cup, they collapse and leave the organic matter in the cup.

Ion exchange: Think of ion exchange as a process in which an ionized molecule is bonded to an oppositely charged surface. A polar molecule has both positive and negative charges that are balanced within the molecule, but the molecule will orient its more negative or positive side to the oppositely-charged site in a filter media. When a charged molecule touches a surface having an opposite charge, a

chemical bond (known as an ionic bond) holds the molecule firmly attached to the surface. The media used are zeolite clays or ion-exchange resins. One reason for the name is that an ion is released from the medium

Both hard corals and soft corals are greatly affected by the buildup of dissolved organic compounds that chemical filtration processes are designed to remove. Photo by U. Erich Friese.

The same biological processes that occur in the aquarium occur also in outdoor ponds, and usually on a much larger scale even if more slowly. Pond owners have available to them a wide range of filtration devices, but fewer than indoor aquarists. Photo by Guido Lurquin.

FILTRATION EQUIPMENT

BIOLOGICAL FILTERS

Under this heading I am grouping the filters whose primary objective is to provide biological filtration. The fact is that many mechanical filters also provide some biological filtration after they have been in operation for a while. I am referencing biological filters as those devices that have been designed for the primary purpose of breaking down ammonia, a major metabolite of all animals. Nearly all biological filters work with the help of our old friends, those "true rulers," the bacteria. For that reason, it helps get things started to add a little gravel or water from an established aquarium (in order to "seed" the new tank with beneficial bacteria).

Undergravel Filter

This is the "granddaddy" of all biological filters that have been used in aquaria. It is interesting to note that several decades ago there were only two books that devoted themselves to the saltwater aquarium—and they gave contrary advice as regards filtration! In retrospect, this is not difficult to understand. One advocated utilizing an outside power filter and not to use any gravel at all. The idea was to keep down the bacteria count in order to maintain the pH in the aquarium, an historic problem with marine aquaria. It sounded good, but the other book advocated an undergravel filter, and it

turned out that it was this method that was most successful, for the undergravel filter becomes a biological filter as soon as the gravel is colonized by nitrifying bacteria. Who could have believed that actually encouraging bacteria in the marine aquarium would have been a good thing?

One of the problems with the undergravel filter, though, was that it became clogged with detritus that was not recycled quickly enough. One solution to this was to siphon out and clean the gravel at regular intervals but to clean only part of it at a time so that the beneficial bacteria were left. (Also, regular "vacuuming" of the gravel helped.) Another was to keep the particulate matter separate from the undergravel filter. This was done by a reverse-

flow undergravel filter. The water was mechanically filtered before being pumped up through the gravel bed.

It is only the latter type of undergravel filter that should be utilized in a marine reef tank. But the fact is that most reef "tankers" (i.e. reef tank keepers) don't utilize gravel at all. Or, if they do, they utilize living sand. The problem is that all of the base rock covers the sand and makes it difficult to clean with a vacuum or siphon hose with an adapter. Even I am inclined not to use an undergravel filter in a reef tank—not even a reverse-flow one—but it is always a possible choice for freshwater tanks, as well as fish-only marine tanks. And, besides that, it has had an important history as the first fully biological filter in the freshwa-

A reverse flow undergravel filter system being powered by a canister filter. Here the direction of water flow is the opposite of that in a traditional undergravel filter, with water being pushed up and through the filter bed from below. A power source to create water circulation at the top of the tank is also being used here. Drawing by John Quinn.

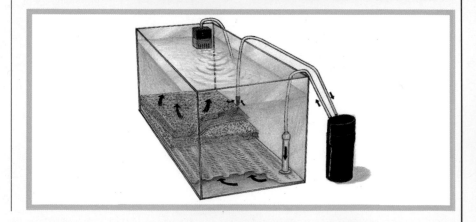

ter and marine aquarium hobby.

Powerheads

Powerheads are not actually filters, but they are used to drive filters. They are particularly recommended for the undergravel filter. A powerhead will move a much greater volume of water than just airstones on the lift tubes. Even more important, powerheads are presently constructed that can provide reverse-flow filtration on an undergravel filter. They have a small mechanical filter, either a sponge or fiber pad, that

Attaching a powerhead to an undergravel filter. Photo by I. Francais.

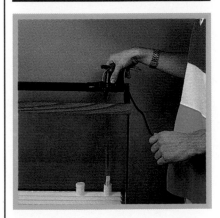

filters out solid debris and keeps the particulate matter separate from the biological filtration, as is recommended. Powerheads often now are able to provide aeration by continuously releasing bubbles of air into the water, and these units are much recommended.

Trickle Filters

These filters are also known as wet/dry filtration. This is the system which had everyone so excited just a few years ago. Results were spectacular compared with what we had experienced before. The filter is primarily a biological filter, so the water should be prefiltered for this device as well. Most of the commercial wet/dry filters have a prefilter built into the intake, even if it is only a sponge filter. (I say "only," but actually sponge filters are quite effective *if they are cleaned on a regular and frequent basis.* Cleaning should consist of scrubbing and rinsing the sponge in some aquarium water which has been siphoned out for the purpose. The reason for using the aquarium water is to preserve the bacteria which will inhabit a sponge filter and provide some biological filtration. Naturally, no detergent or soap should be utilized in the cleaning. The sponge should then be replaced and the aquarium water discarded.) Most wet/dry filters have a skimmer for taking water from the aquarium. These can be adjusted so that the surface of the water doesn't show. In my opinion, that should be done. As a long-time hobbyist, seeing the surface of the water is tacky; it makes it look as though replacement water has not been used to compensate for evaporation. Incidentally, these surface skimmers are equipped with a siphon-proof system to keep your water from siphoning out on the floor in case the pump stops from an electrical outage, or whatever reason. Such fine touches are truly appreciated by those of us who live with glass houses.

The reason wet/dry filters are often referred to as "trickle" filters is that not many commercial models have incorporated the wet part of the wet/dry filtration, or, at most, it is only a small part of the filter. The idea was to improve upon the undergravel filter by maximizing the amount of oxygen exposure to the bacteria so that the filter would function more efficiently. A further

Trickle filtration is one of the techniques employed to provide maximum oxygenation and large surface area for the beneficial bacteria on which biological filtration systems depend. Trickle filter systems are available in units that either hang on the tank or are placed separately; some units are equipped with built-in protein skimmers. Photo courtesy of Ultra Life Reef Products.

The filtration system employed in this minireef aquarium is a relatively large and complicated compound system that is effectively hidden in the customized stand holding the tank. The unit is being lighted by a metal halide lamp. Photo by Cheng,

purpose was to increase the exchange of gases.

The dry part of the filter, then, consists of a tray of inert porous material, such as clay granules, and a spray bar covers the material evenly (as evenly as it can possibly be designed to do so) with water from the tank. A dry filter can be suspended above the tank, with the water simply trickling over the medium, and the shallow flow of the water allows for good gas exchange. The bacteria function up to 20 times as efficiently when utilized in this manner. Of course, there is no wet part to such a filter; nevertheless, devices just described have been quite popular—especially in Europe.

Another approach is to use what is commonly called a tower, and this has been the most common method of the commercial wet/dry filters. The medium for "housing" the bacteria is what are commonly called "bio-balls." These are plastic spheres with as many surfaces as possible for the desirable bacteria. That is, they are hollow and have irregular openings to the interiors. A drip plate or spray bar is placed over the tower, and the water is taken from the aquarium and run through the tower at not too fast a rate. This again provides the exposure to the air that is desirable. The only problem is that a tower is enclosed, so the air can become stagnant. For that reason, a flow of air is pumped upward (counter to the flow of water) or openings in the tower are provided for ventilation. (Remember I commented earlier that all the biological filters would take into account the bacteria's need for oxygen to do a good job? This is one of those times.)

Another medium utilized in a tower is coiled plastic matting. This material has lots of air spaces, so it satisfies the requirement for the water's being exposed to lots of air for a good exchange of gases. Almost always a rotating spray bar is utilized in a tower with coiled matting, as the roundness of the matting is matched by the circular distribution of water by the spray bar. The spray bar is turned by the force of the water itself, as the holes are placed strategically so that the water leaving the spray bar imparts motion to it, much like many garden hose sprinklers.

Whether plates of sand or ceramic material or plastic matting is used, the water eventually gets down to the "wet" part of the wet/dry filter. Now the idea behind the wet portion of the filter is to utilize anaerobic, or non-

A closeup of bioballs in use in one chamber of a wet/dry filter. The many convolutions and interstices in each ball greatly increase the surface area that can be colonized by beneficial bacteria.

oxygen using, bacteria for breaking down nitrates.

At its simplest, such a filter consists of an inert medium, preferably porous, and the chamber should be kept dark (to avoid competition from algae), and there should be a low water turnover. The last requirement is what has made it difficult to incorporate the wet portion of the wet/dry filter with the dry trickle filter. The movement of water through the dry system is too fast for the movement of water through the wet section. Compromises are made, and many manufacturers include a wet section in the sump of the trickle filter. The sump is of fairly good size in these cases, and that gives the water time to "sit" while waiting for the sump pump to return the water to the aquarium. This allows the anaerobic bacteria to at least have some time for breaking down nitrates. The problem is that the water entering the sump is very well oxygenated. One way for getting around this problem is to have a very deep medium so that the bacteria can thrive at the bottom. Still, the wet portion of the filter generally seems to function better separately, and denitrators have been invented that actually work—but more about them later. In any case, the denitrators are often placed in the sump, or wet portion, of the wet/dry filter.

The sump is where all the water collects beneath the trays, bioballs, or matting. A pump in this area returns the water to the tank. The sump is a handy place for placing protein skimmers (in marine tanks), and it is a handy place to place bags of activated

carbon to provide chemical filtration.

It should be mentioned that freshwater hobbyists who utilize trickle filtration are usually not concerned about the denitrator section of the filter, as there is much reliance in the freshwater hobby on frequent partial water changes to dilute any nitrate buildup.

Compound Filters

Although, as we have seen, the various filters and devices often have their own idiosyncratic requirements as to water flow, the convenience of having everything incorporated into one flow system has inspired manufacturers to produce wet/dry filters that have everything contained within them—even the heater. Such devices have a cup-like take-up system from the aquarium that skims water from the surface (where the most organic compounds are likely to be), and runs the water through some mechanical filter medium, such as nylon wool, then goes to a drip plate or rotating spray bar, then through bioballs, coiled matting, or other inert material, then through a chemical filter, and then into the sump, in which there may be a protein skimmer as well as a wet filter medium.

There are disadvantages to such a compound filter, of course. The main problem is that nearly every unit is compromised somewhat because of the requirements of the others. For example, it would be best to have the mechanical and chemical filter placed before the inlet to the trickle filter, but the flow would be too fast for that class of filter. As it is, of

A minireef tank with an extensive array of support equipment, all accommodated on a rack of 2 x 4s bolted for strength and stability. Installations like this are often used for aquaria viewable through plasterboard and other easily notched-out walls. Photo by John Burleson.

course, the flow is too fast for the maximum performance of the wet portion of the filter. And a protein skimmer needs a "crack" at the water before any filtration at all! Nevertheless, the convenience of this setup outweighs the problems in the opinion of many hobbyists.

BIO-WHEELS

The bio-wheel is a device that has been designed to provide wet/dry filtration for a tank of any size with a simple-but-ingenious device. Usually incorporated in an outside filter, the bio-wheel consists of a rotating "wheel" that is composed of porous material, an ideal medium for beneficial bacteria to colonize. The wheel turns through the water (providing the "wet" part of the filtration) and then turns up out of the water for the dry part. During the dry part of the filtration the water is spread out thinly on the bio-wheel, so the bacteria get

their much-needed oxygen, which enables them to work more efficiently.

The beauty of the bio-wheel filters is that they provide wet/dry filtration for aquaria that are generally too small to consider for a regular wet/dry unit. As a point of fact, bio-wheels provide wet/dry biological filtration for all types of aquaria, as there are large units for larger aquaria. The rotating bio-wheel provides up to ten times more biological filtration than a regular power filter of similar size. The wet/dry design increases gas exchange, removes more toxic ammonia and nitrite, and reduces the biological oxygen demand from the tank water, leaving more oxygen for the tank inhabitants. In addition, many of the devices are quite cleverly designed to have only one moving part, a silent magnetic impeller. Power filters equipped with bio-wheels provide all three types

of filtration, mechanical, chemical, and biological, as the filter can be equipped with cartridges for mechanical filtration and packets of activated carbon for the much-desired chemical component.

An alternative configuration for the bio-wheel is to utilize an especially large one—or series of large ones—in line with a canister filter. The idea here is the time-honored one of keeping the particulate matter separate from the biological filter. The canister filter supplies the mechanical filtration, and the bio-wheel provides the biological filtration.

Fluidized Bed Biological Filters

This is a relatively new system, but everything that I have experienced and all my discussions with people and all my readings indicate that this new system is a very fine biological filter. It consists of a bed of filter medium that is kept in a state of constant movement, with a good portion of it being suspended in the water. There is a built-in pump that directs a spray or sprays of water at a strategic point or points, and the filter medium (usually fine beach sand) is contained in a holder shaped like an upside-down pyramid. (Some recent designs involve utilizing a cylindrical shape. In fact, the first time I saw one, I thought that it was a new type of protein skimmer, at first glance.) If nothing else, fluidized biological filters are fun to watch. While not actually new, it has taken some time for them to be properly sized and adapted to the home aquarium. We are finally at the stage at which this type of filter is recognized as one of the alternatives.

One of the main points of this device is that all the filter medium is utilized and is active in the process of biological filtration. (It is worth noting here that, of course, the sand merely provides a "home" for the beneficial bacteria. What this filter does is provide the bacteria equal exposure to any nutrients available.) An important point here is that "dead spots" are virtually non-existent and that the fluidized bed biological filters seem to need virtually no maintenance.

These filters are currently being manufactured to draw water from the sump of the wet/dry filter or from the return tube of a canister filter. (Many hobbyists who are completely sold on fluidized bed filtration use it in place of trickle filtration.) What is worth noting here is that the water should be filtered before being introduced to the fluidized filter. This filter functions mainly as a biological filter, not a mechanical one. But its biological filtering powers are astounding.

One of the most significant problems with any conventional biological filter is that the layers of bacteria that accumulate on the surface of the media can get quite thick, thereby blocking the transfer of nutrients and oxygen to the lower layers. In time, this results in a mature and thick colony of bacteria that consume fewer nutrients than a younger, thinner culture. Because of the constant movement of the medium, there is a constant sloughing of older layers of bacteria,

Fluidized bed filters achieve a high degree of effectiveness among biological filtration devices by greatly increasing the surface area of the filter medium on which aerobic bacteria can live and providing the oxygen-rich environment they require. Some fluidized bed filters also allow for a degree of chemical and mechanical filtration. Photo courtesy of Wardley Corporation.

which ensures that those present are younger and more efficient "converters."

Fluidized bed biological filters have more surface area than any other type of biological filter. Because of this, they can be compactly designed. There is virtually no maintenance involved. In short, these fluidized filters can handle just about anything. They do more work, cost less, and require less maintenance than all other biological filters.

Water may be introduced into one of these filters by two methods. You can utilize a small powerhead from the sump in your wet/dry filter or you can add a T-fitting into the return line from your main pump and divert part of the water flow to the inlet valve, using the attached valve to regulate the flow into the filter. (There is a limit to the amount of water that can be processed through the filter.) Modern units are now being manufactured that can

hang on the aquarium and take the water directly from the tank. Such units have their own prefilters, and they are quite simple to utilize.

About the only disadvantage of the fluidized bed filters is that the bacteria function so well that they take up a lot of oxygen. For that reason and the fact that no mechanical filtration takes place in this system, these filters are now often a part of another system. That is, a fluidized filter may be incorporated in a compound filter or in a canister filter. Such systems address the problems of sieving out suspended matter and of oxygenating the water.

Algae Scrubbers

This, again, is a type of device that is primarily used for marine aquaria, but, again, that is because marine hobbyists are so intent on eliminating the buildup of nitrate and prolonging the time between water changes.

Algae scrubbers are often called algal turf scrubbers, and they have their adherents. The scrubbers are basically shallow troughs with a plastic mesh screen. Water is often pumped to the troughs by means of a "dump bucket" to simulate waves. The waves help the algae to exchange gases, as they are exposed to the air in between surges. The various turf-forming algae that grow on the screens remove ammonia, nitrate, phosphate, and heavy metals from the water. The screens have to be serviced periodically by removing them and scraping off the excess algal growth with a plastic scraper.

Of course, the troughs are under intense lighting. One of the problems has been to design systems that fit well on home aquaria, as the system was first developed and utilized by Dr. Walter Adey at the Smithsonian Institution's natural history museum in Washington. Hang-on models that fit on the back of an aquarium are available, as are large units that can service a

number of aquaria. Molded models are now available that can fit any size system. They can be installed above, behind, or below tanks.

It is interesting to note that very few people are ambivalent about algae scrubbers. Hobbyists either love them or hate them. Obviously, many hobbyists have had good success with them. Very few of even the most ardent turf scrubber advocates are in favor of using the algae scrubbers as the sole method of treating the water. While the algae scrubbers do a good job of removing various undesirable substances, they also release dissolved organic compounds (DOC) into the water, which can give the water a yellowish cast. The use of a protein skimmer can take care of this problem, and bags of activated carbon will help, too.

The Denitrator

This is a device that has been much dreamed about but has only recently become a reality. One of the problems encountered during attempts

made to utilize porous rock into which anaerobic bacteria could eventually colonize the centers was that the flow of water was too fast and tended to inhibit the colonization of anaerobic bacteria, as oxygen is lethal to them. Another concern was that toxic gases would be released into the water and harm or kill the invertebrates and fish.

The denitrators are ingenious devices that are airtight and take in water at a very slow rate. The outflow sits above the water level and puts out water at a very slow rate, but the nitrate has been eliminated by the anaerobic bacteria. There is a venting device in the denitrator so that any toxic gases are vented into the atmosphere and not into the water. The fact is, though, that the device has been designed so that denitrification takes place slowly enough that noxious gases should not be produced. With nitrate being taken out of the water, partial water changes can be even less frequent. The denitrator is a promising bit of new equipment, and it is being seen as a component of more and more reef systems. Speaking of components, it is time to discuss some devices that are not, strictly speaking, biological filters.

MECHANICAL FILTERS

Again, there is going to be some "fudging" here, as some mechanical filters also give us at least a little bit of biological filtration and chemical filtration. Still, let us take a look at what is available.

Inside Box Filters

The simplest representative of this type of filter is the air-

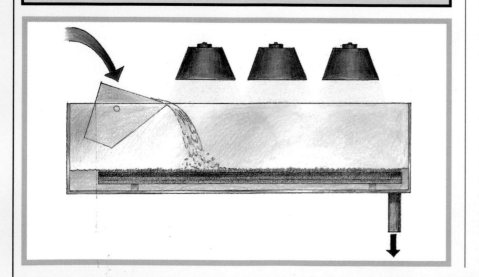

An algae scrubber, showing the bright light source and the action of the dump bucket, which receives water from the tank. Drawing by John Quinn.

The inside box filter in this tank is working in conjunction with the tank's undergravel filter system by helping to trap suspended material, thereby reducing the amount of organic matter that could be drawn into the gravel. Photo by I. Francais.

driven box filter. It consists of a plastic container, a platform for holding the filtering material, and an airstone for lifting the water from underneath the platform. By removing the water, a downward current is created to draw the aquarium water through the filtering material in the box. The filtering material usually consists of glass wool or plastic filter floss, which is intended to collect the large particles of debris in the water. Underneath the filter floss is very likely activated carbon. The efficiency of the carbon can vary, but a high grade of carbon will remove not only organic matter but also some metals and gases. In fact, when a tank is being medicated, filters containing activated carbon are removed, as they will filter out medications, too. (The activated carbon part of the filter would then be providing chemical filtration.)

In the same way that the undergravel filter was historically the workhorse of mechanical filters, being simple and inexpensive, the box filter has been the workhorse of mechanical filters. It is versatile and inexpensive, and it can be moved from tank to tank. For example, it can be used in a new tank to avoid new tank syndrome, because it will filter out organics and, at the same time, help seed the new tank with a colony of nitrifying bacteria. (Of course, this last part will work only if the filter has been used previously in a well established aquarium.) And it should be noted once again that the box filter can become a biological filter, as the filter box and the carbon become colonized by nitrifying bacteria. Once again, it is advisable to change the filter material regularly, as the organic matter trapped in the carbon is still in contact with the water. Also, activated carbon loses its effectiveness in a relatively short time (in a few days, sometimes) so it needs to be replenished, too.

It may be noticed that there are conflicting interests here. On the one hand, we want to change the filter to get rid of the organic matter and to replenish the supply of activated carbon. On the other, when we clean the filter, we are getting rid of the colony of nitrifying bacteria that have been doing beneficial work for the tank. One way around this problem is to have two inside filters in the tank and change them on alternating schedules. That way, one of the filters is always providing some biological filtration.

Inside Power Filters

The main difference between the inside power filter and the inside box filter is that the inside power filter is likely to be larger, and it is powered by an electrical motor which runs the water through the filter quite rapidly. Because of the larger capacity of such a filter, it can filter a larger tank and go longer between changes of the filter element and cleaning of the filter. The disadvantage of all inside filters is that they are not out of sight and may annoy hobbyists who want a completely natural display. However, a little innovation can arrange for such filters to be hidden behind rockwork. Of course, this means that the rocks must be removed before the filter, but a little pain is good for the soul. Besides, the true hobbyist enjoys all of these little chores!

Sponge filters, obtainable in different sizes and shapes, work both biologically and mechanically to remove impurities and are especially useful in aquaria holding fish fry or other tiny organisms that would be in danger of being sucked into other types of filters. Photo courtesy of Jungle Laboratories Corporation.

on a regular basis. An outside filter is going to have many of the components of the inside filter, with filter floss and activated carbon being typical materials. An outside air-driven filter usually requires a more powerful air pump than an inside box filter requires, because the water must be lifted either out of the aquarium or back into it.

Power Filters

Think of a power filter as an outside filter with a motor on it, for that is just what it is. Naturally it can run the water through the filter much more quickly, so the filter can be much larger, and more filtering material will be needed for processing more water. Also, the siphon tubes, which usually carry the water

Inside Foam Filters

Inside foam filters are designed to eventually be biological filters, but they function as mechanical filters until the foam becomes colonized by the desired bacteria. They are inexpensive and handy, much like inside box filters, and they, too, can be moved around from tank to tank.

Outside Air-Driven Filters

Just think of the outside air-driven filter as a box filter that hangs on the back of the aquarium. The advantages are that it can be kept pretty much out of sight and can be larger, since it is not taking up any room in the tank. It is also easier to clean without disrupting the tank. This is truly a major advantage, for the simple truth is that the easier a filter is to clean, the more likely it is to be cleaned

Closeup of the action in one version of an air-powered outside filter. Water is taken from the tank by gravity action after the flow has started and allowed to flow downward through the filter floss and carbon in the compartment at right in the filter box. It then enters the smaller compartment at left and is pumped back with the air bubbles rising through the return stem. Photo by M. F. Roberts.

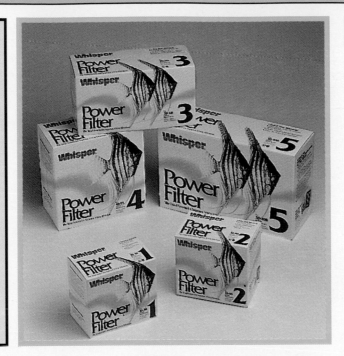

Power filters provide mechanical and chemical filtration and also achieve a degree of biological filtration as well; they are easy to maintain. Photo courtesy Tetra/Second Nature.

into the filter, will be much larger. That is because the filter will pump (or release, in the case of waterfall-style filters) water back into the aquarium quite fast, so two large siphon tubes will sometimes be needed.

The power filter has the same advantages as the outside air-driven filter except that it processes more water. For that reason, it can service a larger tank. The only disadvantage that I can think of is that the siphon tubes can be so large that a special adapter has to be used for holding the water in the siphon tube as you put it into the filter.

Canister Filters

The canister filter is the darling of today's hobbyists. The advantage to this device is that it pumps the water under pressure. That way the water can be processed much faster than by even an outside power filter. Technically, of course, the canister filter *is* an outside filter and is powered, too; it is simply the

evolution of that type of filter into its most advantageous form. The water is removed rapidly out of the tank and run through the filter media, then returned to the tank. Often it is returned via a spray bar, which provides the

aeration that might otherwise have been missing. Besides, the rapid turnover of water keeps the water in the tank circulating so that there is a more efficient gas exchange at the surface, for all of the water is eventually circulated there, and it happens more quickly with a canister filter. A further advantage of the canister filter is that, since the water is under pressure, it will not go around the filter media as it begins to clog up with material.

The reader may be able to see here why I tried to simplify things by dividing the filters into only biological and mechanical filters. Whenever filters have activated carbon in them, they are also partly chemical filters. The tip-off was when I discussed how activated carbon removes dissolved gases and organic compounds. Now to complicate things even further,

In addition to their overall effectiveness at being able to provide a combination of mechanical, biological and chemical filtration, canister filters also can be hidden out of sight if their owner so chooses. Photo courtesy Eheim/Hawaiian Marine.

canister filters not only are able to provide mechanical and chemical filtration, they also are designed to do biological filtration. In fact, some units are big enough to offer a wet/dry system in a single canister that can be easily fitted into a cabinet or shelf beneath the tank. Hence, canister filters could be covered under biological, mechanical, or chemical filtration. The fact is that many units do all three.

The canister filter units that are designed for mechanical filtration usually arrive with a large supply of activated carbon. That is to remove the organic matter until the tank is sufficiently mature that it can provide the filter with the beneficial bacteria for biological filtration. Even after the transformation has been made, there still is a compartment for activated carbon.

The only disadvantage to canister filters is that there must be some relatively unsightly tubing that goes

into the tank to transport the water in and out of the tank, but even this has been so simplified that it can't be called much of a disadvantage.

Diatomaceous Earth Filters

Diatoms are single-celled algae that live in colonies and are encased in microscopic two-valved frustules (shells) made of silica. There are over ten thousand species of diatoms, but the tiny pores in the silica frustules will filter out all but the tiniest particles. Many species have frustules with pores that are quite uniform in size. Diatomaceous earth is made up of sediments of the ancient silica shells of diatoms, and it is widely used as a filtration media in swimming pools. There are also diatomaceous earth filters that are used for home aquaria. They do an excellent job of "polishing" the water, as they will filter out particles so small that they can't be seen but nevertheless can cloud the water if there

are enough of them. For that reason, they can interfere with the clarity of the water. The diatom units remove all of this to the extent that the fish seem suspended in air, so clear is the water.

Most diatomaceous earth filters have their own motors and are sealed units so that they can be moved from one aquarium to another. It is difficult to use one of these filters as a permanent filter, as they are so efficient that the filter becomes clogged after only a little over an hour of use in most tanks. In fact, they will become clogged just from the protective slime molecules from the fish. They must then be cleaned, "recharged" with diatomaceous earth, and returned to use. Of all the strictly mechanical filters, this is one of the most efficient.

CHEMICAL FILTRATION

When we speak of chemical filtration, we normally are talking about the use of activated carbon. Activated carbon started out as organic matter of some sort, usually bone or coconut shell. Whichever it is, it doesn't matter. It is treated with chemicals to dehydrate it, and then it is heated in a series of steps, first without air and then in the presence of steam. The so-called "activation" process creates pores and removes organic matter from pores that already exist. A good grade of activated carbon has a tremendous amount of surface area. Some grades have a total surface area of 2000 meters per gram. That is because of all of the tiny pores in each granule. Since high grades of activated carbon are made up of tiny grains, marine hobbyists often refer to it by the initials GAC, for granular activated carbon. (There are a lot of acronyms in the aquarium hobby. Learning them is a rite of passage!)

Activated carbon (or GAC) will remove dissolved organic compounds (DOC!), noxious gases, and, yes, even trace elements in a marine tank. But that is okay. Marine aquarists add trace elements for a number of reasons, one of them being that the organisms in the tank absorb them. Because activated carbon removes trace elements, marine hobbyists were slow to take to it. However, it is commonplace now. One reason for that is that it is the best way to cure or prevent a yellowish cast to the water developing from the dissolved organic compounds in the water.

Protein Skimmers

Some hobbyists may be surprised to find the protein skimmer here, as the process certainly seems mechanical. Just remember that protein skimming is an action upon organic molecules at the molecular level, and that makes it a chemical filter— even if it doesn't involve activated carbon. The process falls under the category of adsorption.

The protein skimmer is sometimes called a water fractionator, and it works on the principle that it is easy to create bubbles in ocean water, and there is a collection of organic material at the surface of those bubbles. If the bubbles are collected in a cup or have an overflow to dispose of them, organic molecules can be removed even before they become part of the nitrogen cycle. In other words, one of the main advantages of the protein skimmer is that it greatly reduces the load on your biological filter. So efficient are many protein skimmers that they have become quite popular with marine aquarists, from fish enthusiasts to invertebrate devotees to living reef connoisseurs.

One reason that the protein skimmer is so often mentioned first among the auxil-

One type of protein skimmer. Photo by V. Serbin.

iary equipment available is that it can be so effective and can really help you keep the redox potential of your tank up there where you want it. Because the protein skimmer pulls the organics out of the water before they have a chance to break down into harmful components, it takes a load off your undergravel filter and off your mechanical and chemical filters, too. The disadvantage is that it is a further complication, and it is a device that needs daily attention. The air bubbles have to be just right, and the cup should be emptied daily. The device should be monitored daily, too, to be sure that the foam is going into the cup or overflow device at the right consistency. You don't want to be losing your water, and you don't want the bubbles sliding right back into the tank again.

It will take time working with your device for you to get to the point that you are truly proficient at having the protein skimmer work at its best. It is difficult to designate a specific bubble size, but a profusion of small bubbles is generally preferred. However, if the bubbles are too small, the foam may not form properly, or the bubbles may be less persistent. If the bubbles are too large, they rise too quickly through the tube and the discharge is too watery. A little experimentation will help you decide what size bubble and rate of flow is best for your system.

Some excellent protein skimmers are available. I prefer the venturi pump-driven protein skimmers, which are nearly always situated outside the tank. There are also some excellent counter-current skimmers designed for use outside the tank. The water goes to the protein skimmer and back to the tank via the power of the pump in the protein skimmer. Protein skimmers designed for use inside the tank are generally less expensive, but they are more difficult to service (which you have to do daily), and the water level in the tank becomes a crucial factor. (Some inside skimmers are on brackets so that you can adjust the skimmer to the water level, but that is a pain, too).

Besides the fact that an inside protein skimmer takes away from the natural look of the aquarium, its height is limited by that of the tank. That affects its efficiency, as the higher the tube the longer the bubbles are in contact with the water and the more efficient your protein-skimming operation. Manufacturers and hobbyists have done work with inside protein skimmers, though, and some have been devised for sitting inside the sump of a trickle filter or of a compound setup or even an outside filter. That way they are out of sight, and some designs are quite stocky, so their many bubbles help compensate for a lack of height. Still, although an

outside skimmer is more expensive, it has a lot to recommend it, with its higher efficiency and ease of service. And a venturi-driven protein skimmer is the most efficient of all, because of the excellent contact time and the uniform bubble size. (Bubble size is important, because if the bubbles are too large their added buoyancy makes them rise more quickly, thereby reducing contact time. Conversely, bubbles that are too small are not buoyant enough for efficient foam collection.)

Whatever problems a protein skimmer of whatever design might have, it is worth commenting here that it has become the single most important piece of equipment for many marine hobbyists. In fact, many mini-reef hobbyists utilize only the protein skimmer.

The disadvantages to the protein skimmer are few, but they are there. The cup must be checked daily. They can be utilized only on marine

aquaria, as fresh water is not dense enough to make good foam. And the device can remove trace elements. All of these disadvantages can be taken into account and compensated for, but the hobbyist should be aware of them.

Ozonizers

Ozone is the compound that we want in the ozone layer, but we don't want down here on earth. It is a component of smog, created by the reaction of organic compounds with ultraviolet rays (and, yes, an ultraviolet sterilizer does create a little of it), and it is a major contributor to the burning eyes that we experience in severe smog. It causes that sensation because the compound is unstable, consisting of three atoms of oxygen when it is normal for oxygen atoms to associate in pairs. Hence, one of the oxygen atoms breaks free and combines with organic compounds in a process known as oxidation. While this is not beneficial for us, it is quite harmful to bacteria and parasites. Unfortunately, the ozone doesn't discriminate between the good and bad bacteria, and it can also harm the delicate membranes of the fish, such as the gill filaments. It also can injure the tissues of the invertebrates.

Since the ozone gas is a non-selective "killer," the units that draw the water out of the tank and inject the gas into a contact chamber are the ones recommended, and I particularly like those having an activated carbon filter in the

A protein skimmer is visible in the sump area at the right side of this wet/dry filter system. Photo by Cheng.

return lines, as that helps contain the ozone in the reaction chamber.

The ozone sterilizer complicates your system, but it has its beneficial aspects, for not only does it help keep down the bacterial and parasite population, it helps increase the redox potential of the tank by breaking down the molecules of organic compounds. A relatively recent innovation has been to incorporate an ozone generator as part of some of the more fancy protein skimmers.

Ion Exchange Filters

Home units are primarily for removing minerals and metals from the tap water before it is placed into the tank. The disadvantage is that a sodium ion is exchanged for the ion that is removed. Hence, the water may be soft for the purposes of washing clothes, but it isn't the same with water organisms. Some units now combine ion-exchange filtration with absorption and oxidation, and they do an excellent job of preparing the water for the aquarium. They are usually sold as tap water purifiers.

Reverse Osmosis Units

These units would seem not to be chemical, but they

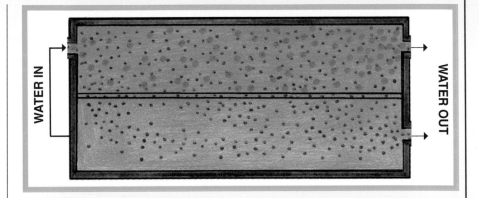

Above: How the reverse osmosis process operates. The water entering the unit is under pressure and contains pollutants (blue circles) that are too large to pass through the immensely fine membrane (thin line centered horizontally in unit), but the pure water molecules (pink circles) are allowed through. Drawing by John Quinn.

Right: Freshwater hobbyists use reverse osmosis systems primarily for obtaining soft water for use with softwater fishes like discus; in the saltwater end of the hobby, they're used mainly to obtain mineral-free water intended for being mixed with artificial sea salts. Photo by B. Degen.

work on the molecular level. The idea is to put water under pressure and force it through a semi-permeable membrane. In this manner, dissolved organics and minerals are filtered out. This is an excellent method of providing pure water for mixing synthetic salt water or for providing water that has had the phosphates and minerals removed for use in freshwater aquaria. Only freshwater fishes that come from extremely softwater areas are likely to need such water. Even so, the water should be mixed with some tap water (probably about 10-15%) to provide the needed minerals. The truth is that even softwater-loving freshwater fish can't live in pure fresh water!

The disadvantage of reverse osmosis units is that they work slowly to produce water, and they take several gallons of tap water to produce one of pure water. Also, the units are relatively expensive. Nevertheless, breeders of discus and keepers of marine aquaria often have these units as standard equipment.

RECOMMENDATIONS

Please be aware that canister filters and power filters, not to mention inside filters, could just as easily be listed under chemical filtration as under mechanical. I have already pointed out that the canister filter could be listed under all three, and this is true to some degree with inside filters and power filters, too. There are so many qualifications to recommending a specific filter that it is best to match a filter to a specific

tank of a particular type. We'll do that in the next chapter.

A NEW DEVELOPMENT

I would be derelict not to mention an exciting new filtration method that may revolutionize the aquarium hobby. The claims seem too good to be true, but they have been verified by reputable sources. As I write this, certain aspects of the filter are in the process of being patented. It is therefore quite new to the aquarium world and is a byproduct of efforts by scientists and technologists to deal with certain environmental problems, such as oil spills and waste disposal. Such efforts have resulted in "designer" bacteria that will consume oil and other noxious products. The new filtration involves the use of a carefully selected mix of bacteria so that anaerobic organisms are not present. It employs a special blend of pelletized carbon.

Although the new system may not replace all the filtration methods described in this publication, it certainly goes a long way toward supplanting them. There are a couple of fantastic aspects to this new filter. First, it cycles tanks in 24 hours. That is, the bacteria are up and running so fast that the ammonia is broken down fast enough that the fish are unharmed. Also, nitrates (NO3) are broken down aerobically by the bacteria and in combination with the special blend of activated carbons, there is no danger to the fish, as the byproducts are vented harmlessly as nitrogen gas. The beauty of

this filtration is that you can get by with adding more fish to the tank than normally would be possible.

I myself saw a living reef tank using this system. This reef tank was the only one I ever saw in which the tank actually looked like a real in-the-ocean-reef, with an abundance of fishes. the fishes had to be selected only in regard to their not feeding on the corals. Other than that, it was completely natural—and spectacular!

Another advantage of this filter is that it can be set up in various configurations. I can be as simple as a box filter or as complex as a trickle filter. It can also be adapted to function equally well in all types of ponds and in freshwater, brackish water, marine tanks and brine tanks. Not only does the filter break down ammonia, nitrite, and nitrate (safely at that!), but it also rids the tank of phosphates, and that pretty much takes care of any problems with troublesome algae.

I am hearing only second-hand about all this, and, as I've said, it sounds too good to be true. But the information is coming from very reputable people, and what a boon it will be for the aquarium hobby. It will no doubt help the growth of the aquarium pursuit, as newcomers will stay with the hobby instead of dropping out because of failure with that first small tank. I look forward to using the product myself when it becomes available commercially, for it truly sounds like a quantum leap forward in the area of aquarium filtration.

SUGGESTED FILTRATION SETUPS

It seems to me that the best thing to do here is to recommend filtration for specific types of tanks. Let's first address freshwater tanks and save the marine systems for last, as they are generally the most complicated.

COMMUNITY TANK

The good old community tank is the one that got most of us hooked on this hobby. It is usually from ten to one hundred gallons in size, and it consists of small fish such as tetras, guppies, swordtails, platies, cory catfish, and numerous other little jewels. Of course, there can be other community tanks, too, such as a cichlid community tank—or even a community tank of killies—but I will deal with some of those communities separately. For now, I am considering only the traditional community tank with its traditional complement of tiny fishes.

Many people think of such a tank as a beginner's tank, and it can rightly be called that, as most of us got hooked on the hobby as a result of seeing someone else's beautiful display. I am also of the opinion that aquarium shop dealers should set up at least one community tank display, as I am certain it would improve their business—and

Community tanks, especially freshwater community tanks set up primarily for display, often contain mostly small fishes such as tetras and some of the smaller barbs, thereby placing less of a load on the filtration system than bigger, chunkier fishes would entail. Photo by Mella Panzella.

For an aquarium in which an undergravel filter is the main source of filtration, the size of the gravel used must be taken into account. When using an undergravel filter, follow the specifications of the manufacturer of the filter as regards gravel size and bed depth. The brown substrate shown here could be too coarse for good undergravel filter efficiency.

get even more people into our hobby! But the point is that such tanks are not only for beginners. Experienced tropical fish hobbyists are the ones who can put together the most beautiful community tanks, and they usually do so.

Even diehard cichlid fans will often have community tanks in the living room of their homes. The question for us at the moment is: what is the best way to filter such tanks?

Obviously, what provides the very best filtration would

be a matter of opinion. There are many experienced hobbyists around the world, and we could get many differing opinions about the best way to filter just the community aquarium, never mind specialized setups. However, I am

Choosing the right type of filtration system(s) and equipment for use in a marine aquarium can be more complicated by virtue of the fact that in many saltwater aquaria there is a much greater variety of different animal groups, each of which might have special requirements. Another consideration is that the fishes and other animals in the marine field in general cost more, often much more, than freshwater tank inhabitants—which in itself should lead marine hobbyists to take their time in deciding upon the best system for them. Photo courtesy of Nancy Aquarium.

reasonably certain that many of them would recommend just what I do. First, it is difficult to fault the good old undergravel filter. It will provide excellent mechanical filtration and will eventually provide good biological filtration. This would be inexpensive, as all you would need would be the air pump, air tubing and valve(s), and the undergravel filter. It would be a good idea to also have a siphon hose with a special adapter for vacuuming the gravel. Remember that one of

the problems of the undergravel filter is that debris tends to accumulate in

the gravel. This can lead to what we call "channeling," meaning that the water flow tends to take the course of least resistance and go around the areas where organic matter has accumulated. Regular vacuuming of the gravel, about once a week, will prevent such problems. A number of devices on the market make the task of vacuuming the gravel much easier—and a good deal less sloppy than it used to be.

If you aren't on a restrictive budget, a more ideal setup would be a reverse-flow undergravel system. This can be set up with powerheads, and the only problem with them is that the mechanical filter incorporated within them will have to be changed on at least a weekly basis. If you do use powerheads, be sure to get the type that provide aeration. An even better setup would be to utilize canister filters. You can get a special hose for placing over the top of the lift tubes of

your undergravel filters. The water flow should be from the tank to the canister filter, out the hose (which usually splits to fit over two lift tubes), and then down the lift tubes and then up through the gravel. An important point here is to not have any free-standing open lift tubes. That is, don't put the canister filter outlet on only one or two lift tubes and have two that are standing idle. The water flow (taking the course of least resistance) would then tend to go up the idle lift tubes rather than up through the gravel.

If the tank is a large one, between fifty gallons and a hundred, or even larger, think in terms of adding some canister filters for running the undergravel filter and providing additional filtration. Now the question becomes what filter material to have in the canister filters. It is actually possible to have the best of both worlds with the canister filters, as there are compartments for activated carbon so

A view into a cabinet housing the canister filters providing filtration for a shallow but very capacious minireef aquarium display in an aquarium store. Some of the filters are hooked up in series, with each canister in the series containing a different filtration medium. Photo by Dr. Herbert R. Axelrod.

Very large aquaria are candidates for biological filtration systems that are themselves comparatively very large in surface area, such as big trickle filter units. Photo by Doshin Kobayashi.

that you can have chemical filtration. But there are also compartments for ceramic "noodles" and other synthetic materials for bacteria to colonize. That way you can actually have all the filtration provided by the undergravel filter, chemical filtration in the canister filters, and an additional biological filter that is also contained in the canister filter. For simplicity's sake— and I am one for always keeping a setup as simple as possible!—you have the option of having one canister filter filled with activated carbon, while the other has the components for biological filtration. That way, you have the best of both worlds of biological and chemical filtration.

If you have a really large community tank, such as in excess of a hundred or two hundred gallons, you might want to think in terms of a wet/dry filter. The fact is that if you are a fan of trickle filtration, you can have it on smaller setups, too. In fact, there are even canister filters that are designed as wet/dry filters, with special designs for prolonging the run of the water over the biological beds and arrangements for providing oxygen to the bacteria. One of the problems with trickle filtration is that usually the gravel is not considered or is eliminated (usually in marine tanks, though). One way around that problem is to utilize a canister filter as a

wet/dry filter and get the adapters for fitting over the lift tubes on the undergravel filter.

If you are growing live plants, you can forgo an undergravel filter, as the plants will tend to take care of some of the biological filtration in the sand and gravel. In that case, you could simply use a canister filter for your basic filtration. But it should be pointed out here that an undergravel filter is not incompatible with plants. The long-standing myth that it is stems from the days when people first used undergravel filtration. They tended to use very large gravel, and they seldom vacuumed it. The very large gravel and the accumu-

Used correctly, undergravel filters can be employed in tanks in which lush growth of rooted plants is desired. Photo by M-P. and C. Piednoir, Aqua Press.

lations of organic matter tended to be detrimental to plants. Although most plant enthusiasts prefer to eschew the undergravel filter, there have been sufficient successes with undergravel filters and plants to prove that the two can work together. This is particularly true of the reverse-flow undergravel filter.

Recommendations

It is difficult to go wrong with either a reverse-flow undergravel filter or a canister filter in these type of tanks. With canister filters running the undergravel filter, you get the best of biological, mechanical, and chemical filtration, so that setup is my personal preference. I use it myself and recommend it to my friends for the community tank of small fishes.

CICHLID TANKS

Probably the most popular area of specialization in the freshwater field these days is the family Cichlidae. These animals have become popular with aquarists because they have extremely interesting behavior, they are among the most colorful of all aquarium fishes, and they are interesting from a biological point of view. They would seem to be perfect aquarium fishes, but they aren't! Not only do most members of the family tend to get too large for the home aquarium, but many species are renowned for their bellicose nature. Not only that, but many of them dig in the gravel, completely incapacitating or severely compromising an undergravel filter. They are such a problem that one would wonder why they are popular if it were not for the fact that they are some of the most interesting and beautiful fish on the planet.

Obviously, an undergravel filter is not recommended for the cichlid tank. Even small specimens tend to dig down to the filter plate of the undergravel filter. Also, larger specimens tend to knock the siphon tubes out of power filters. For that reason, canister filters are the way to go for a cichlid home aquarium. Since cichlids are usually large, trickle filtration is not recommended, as the filter is likely to be overwhelmed by metabolic material. Making regular partial water changes is the way most cichlid hobbyists cope with diluting the metabolites produced by their fishes.

If you keep large and aggressive cichlids in your home aquarium, you may even be faced with specimens that attack the heater and the filter tubes. Fortunately, the newer canister filters have the type of tubing that is difficult

As a group, the dwarf cichlids like the *Apistogramma* above are much less disruptive of the gravel surface than their much larger and more inclined to dig relatives such as the *Herichthys bifasciatus* shown below. Upper photo by Mark Smith; lower photo by M-P. and C. Piednoir, Aqua Press.

to dislodge, but you still may want to set up a grating of some sort to keep your cichlids away from the tubing. The same can be done to protect your heater, but here again, the canister filter may have come to your rescue, as there are models now that contain the heater within the canister filter itself. Not only does this protect the heater from marauding cichlids, but it also is one less thing that needs to be kept in the tank. In addition, some canister filters have a thermometer in them, and all you have to do to read the temperature is to glance at the canister unit.

If you are determined to keep an undergravel filter with your cichlids, it is pos-sible to do. You need to place a level of gravel over the filter plate, then place plastic screening over that. Cut a section of grating (like the grating that is used as fluo-rescent light diffusers) that fits the tank, place another layer of gravel down, put in the grating, and then place more gravel over that. The grating works to prevent the cichlids from successfully digging down past the grating. They can still dig holes, but not very wide or deep ones—which is just what we want!

THE CATFISH AQUARIUM

A new look has appeared in the home aquarium, with catfishes becoming, for the first time, one of the most popular groups in which tropical fish hobbyists like to specialize. This has led to the introduction of the all-catfish home aquarium. Such a setup is likely to have red lights in the reflector rather than the normal wide-spectrum or daylight bulbs. The main reason for that circumstance is that the catfish don't seem to recognize the red lights as anything resembling daylight. The advantage to this is that the catfish species are prima-rily nocturnal. And that is one of the reasons that catfish have become popular—not because they are nocturnal, but because hobbyists have learned how to observe their behavior. Before this period of time, catfishes seemed to

Ameiurus catus **is, like other bullhead catfishes, inclined to grub in the bottom substrate in search of food, but it will do much more digging in a soft bottom than in a gravel bottom. Photo by Aaron Norman.**

One of the reasons for the popularity of the catfishes of the genus *Corydoras* (*Corydoras simulatus* shown here) is that their continual grubbing helps to stir up sediment in the substrate, allowing it to become suspended in the water and removed by mechanical filtration. Photo by Mark Smith.

The glass catfish, *Kryptopterus bicirrhis,* whether maintained singly or in a group, is a mid-water to top-water species that will do no rooting in the substrate at all. Photo by M-P. and C. Piednoir.

simply hide all of the time or to simply be inactive. It is quite fascinating to see their behavior once they think it is night.

There are numerous catfish families, so there is more variation among catfishes than among cichlids, for example, which are only one family. Since there is so much variation, there is not too much that they have in common, but nearly all of them do some foraging along the bottom, with many of them actually probing into the gravel for food. Because of this, it is important to have the gravel be as free of pathogenic bacteria as possible. For that reason, only a reverse-flow undergravel filter is recommended for the catfish aquarium. That way debris is not lodged in the gravel, thereby providing a culture for possibly pathogenic prokaryotes (bacteria).

Again, a canister filter is a good option for the catfish tank, too. It can be used as described earlier to run the undergravel filter or it can be used as the primary filter, with no undergravel filter in the tank. If the latter course is taken, only a thin layer of sand and gravel should be placed in the tank. That way the gravel gets turned over and cleaned regularly by the catfish.

THE TETRA TANK

In case you didn't know it, the family Characidae is in the process of revision, with some changes being made that not all ichthyologists would countenance. For the time being, I am still treating the family as intact and waiting to see what shakes

Peat filtration can be useful in producing the type of water recommended for the keeping and breeding of black neons (*Hyphessobrycon herbertaxelrodi*) and many other small tetra species. Photo by Aaron Norman.

out from all this revision that is going on. In any case, the fishes we are talking about here are the small characins, such as the jewel tetra and the cardinal tetra. These are tiny fishes that certainly helped build the hobby, as their small size and beautiful

appearance have won many converts to the hobby. They are relatively undemanding, but they do best in soft and slightly acid water. One way to get these conditions is to utilize peat moss in the filter. In fact, canister filters have been designed with a peat

One of the advantages offered by these cardinal tetras (*Paracheirodon axelrodi*) and other small characoid species is that they don't put much of a load on an aquarium's filtration system even when maintained in groups large enough to let the fish exhibit their normal social behavior. Photo by H.J. Richter.

moss compartment. The peat moss is usually sold as one of the filter components.

The recommendations for this group of fish are the same as far as filtration goes, except that you may want to include a reverse osmosis unit in your aquarium equipment for softening your tapwater, as your fish will absolutely glow in the kind of water that suits them. Depending on the hardness of your water, try mixing from a quarter to a half of your tapwater with your reverse osmosis water.

It is possible to utilize an undergravel filter with these fish, too, but it takes a little experimentation. The peat has a tendency to soften and acidify the water, which is of course one reason it is used. It also is believed to release some beneficial hormones, but all of that is aquarium lore and has not to my knowledge been proved scientifically. Obviously, if you have a reverse osmosis unit, you will not have as great a need for the peat. One way that softwater fish enthusiasts have used peat as an undergravel filter component is to put plastic screening over the filter plate and place a layer of peat over that. Then the gravel is placed on top of the peat. The peat level is normally an inch thick. Please be advised that peat tends to give the water an amber coloration. Many aquarists do not mind that, but it is obviously an acquired taste. If it is not to your liking, rely more on the reverse osmosis unit for your own water conditioning.

A peat bag has been suspended in one chamber of this filter in a wholesaler's tank housing small tetras. Photo by U. Glaser.

BREEDING TANKS

As one who has been to many fish rooms and fish houses of hobbyists and professionals who were occupied with the breeding of different types of fish species, I have seen many different systems used, including some customized central filters. These were biological filters that were designed to provide filtered water to all of the tanks. One of the problems here is to establish a system that delivers water to the tanks and recovers it. One very popular method is to use a U-shaped siphon tube in each tank so that the water levels are the same in each. With such a system, water can be put into a tank on one end and withdrawn from a tank on the other end. For a central filter, the hobbyist can use one of the heavy-duty canister filters, and that would include one (if the hobbyist desires) that provides wet/dry filtration. Such a system would provide good quality water and cut down on the number of water changes needed.

Here is an interesting fact, however. Of all the setups I have seen, the most common has been one that simply used sponge or inside box filters. The tanks were nearly always bare, with no gravel. The only time gravel was supplied was when the fish needed it for spawning. The secret to this setup is frequent partial water changes. This was usually made easy by being able to siphon water out on the floor or by a special siphoning system, with storage tanks or a special filtering of the tapwater so that it could be added right to the tanks. In other words, the emphasis was on partial water changes rather than on biological filtration.

Having said all of that, however, I should also add that there seems to be a new era dawning with more innovation and biological filtration in the fish room. More hobbyists are using central filtration that provides biological and chemical filtration. Water changes are still very much a part of such a system, even though they may be automated and on a timer.

MARINE TANKS

Fish-only Tanks: The category of marine tanks is an all-too-inclusive one, for there are many types of marine tanks. There is the fish-only tank, and there is the minireef tank, not to mention tanks with specialty fishes, such as triggerfishes, which would need some of the same precautions as have been advocated for the cichlid tank—and then some! Still, let me provide an example of a typical setup.

Let's start with a fish-only tank. Although the minireef tank is rapidly becoming the rage in the marine aquarium world, the fish-only tank is still the most popular. One reason for that is that fish tend to graze upon invertebrates in the home aquarium. For that reason, the hobbyist is limited to the type of fishes

> **Sponge filters are especially useful in bare tanks set up for spawning and in fry tanks, where the danger of sucking the fry into a mechanical filter has to be avoided. Here a pair of discus have laid their eggs on a sponge filter in their breeding tank. Photo by Bernd Degen.**

Fish-only marine aquaria are generally less sophisticated in their filtration requirements than minireef tanks and other aquaria containing a substantial population of invertebrates, even though fishes are heavier eaters and more productive of waste materials. Photo by S. Ruchira.

he or she can keep in a minireef tank and is limited in the number of them that can be kept, too. Most tropical fish hobbyists, including those of the marine variety, are interested in fish species, and coral reef fishes are the most colorful in the world, so it is no wonder that the fish-only tank retains its popularity.

In a marine tank, a certain redundancy is required. Thus, a filtration system that consists of a reverse-flow undergravel filter, with a canister filter driving the flow of water through the undergravel filter, is a very common setup. The canister filter would contain activated carbon to provide chemical filtration to remove dissolved organic compounds (DOC). Most people would also have a couple of airstones in the tank to break up the surface tension and aerate the water. One reason for this is that salt water doesn't hold oxygen as well as fresh water does, and marine fishes are generally quite active and need oxygen.

If a protein skimmer is part of the filtration system, the airstones can be eliminated, as the foaming of the protein skimmer will also take care of aeration. Even so, careful hobbyists are likely to include airstones in even this system, as redundancy is the name of the game in the saltwater hobby. This same penchant for redundancy would make most marine hobbyists use two canister filters for driving the undergravel filter, with one containing activated carbon while the other would have compartments set up for providing biological filtration. This system should work on all sizes of tanks. Just keep in mind that you will need more filtration for larger tanks, so you would be using larger or more canister filters, as well as a larger protein skimmer (or more than one).

A fish's eating preferences can affect more than just the amount of waste it produces for a filter to remove. The *Chaetodon bennetti* above, for example, is one of the butterflyfishes that are markedly destructive of living corals and therefore should not be included in a minireef aquarium, and the triggerfish shown below (*Xanthichthys auromarginatus)* can not only destroy corals but also would have a tendency to eat just about anything else, especially crustaceans, small enough to swallow. Photos by Mark Smith.

Other seahorses besides these *Hippocampus erectus* are inexpert hunters that have a hard time competing against faster-swimming fishes for food. Even when maintained by themselves, they often refuse to eat anything but tiny prey such as brine shrimp wafted past them by currents in the tank. Mechanical filtration that would trap such prey before the seahorses could get to it would have to be turned off during feeding periods. Photo by Mark Smith.

Another alternative is to have wet/dry filtration. In the case of the fish-only tank, it would be supplemental to a reverse-flow filter system powered by canister filters. The only other alternative would be not to have gravel. Please be aware that there are all sorts of redundancies that can be utilized here. For example, a fluidized bed filter of the type that hangs on the back of the aquarium could be utilized to supplement biological filtration. For that matter, a compound filter that contains even a denitrator, as well as a protein skimmer, a wet/dry filter, a mechanical filter, and fluidized bed filtration, could be utilized. In most cases, that would be in addition to the reverse-flow filter.

It is perfectly proper to have a reverse-flow filter powered by powerheads, as long as the powerheads are of the type that provide aeration, too, and as long as the mechanical filter on the reverse-flow powerheads is changed regularly and frequently.

Recommendations

As can be seen, the marine tank is inclined to have more redundancies than a craft in the space program. To be a good marine aquarist, you have to love more than fish. You have to be technophile (a gadget lover), too! My personal preference is a reverse-flow undergravel filter, powered by canister filters containing activated carbon and supplemented by a wet/dry filter.

MINIREEF TANKS

The hobbyists who take up minireef tanks are those who are more interested in the invertebrates of the marine world than in the fish. Of course, I am over-simplifying, as some marine hobbyists keep both fish-only tanks and minireef tanks, but the emphasis in the latter is on the corals, anemones, and clams. The fishes come second, and they must be selected very carefully. It is not difficult to develop an intense interest in marine invertebrates, as they can be beautiful and alien. The usual procedure is to get the invertebrates going well first and only then to add a few fishes. Even though fishes are second-

The dragonet *Synchiropus picturatus,* in contrast to the wrasse *Coris gaimard* shown below, is a good candidate for the minireef aquarium. *Synchiropus* species can be useful in keeping down the population of amphipods in such an aquarium but won't bother other crustaceans, but most wrasse species will eagerly feast on show specimen crustaceans. Upper photo by Dr. Herbert R. Axelrod; lower photo by Mark Smith.

class citizens in a reef tank, some species truly prosper in such setups.

The fact is that it has only been in recent years that the photosynthetic organisms, such as corals, anemones, and *Tridacna* clams, could be kept in the home aquarium. That is because there was not sufficient light to enable the symbiotic algae in the tissues of these organisms to prosper. Now high intensity and actinic lighting is available, although it is both expensive to purchase and to maintain. Still, who would have thought that live corals could be kept alive in a home aquarium as successfully as they are today?

In addition to high-inten-sity and broad-spectrum lighting, super-clean water is necessary to be able to keep corals, anemones, and clams. For that reason, trickle filtration is nearly always used. In addition, the gravel is normally not kept in the tank, although it is possible to do so with a reverse-flow undergravel filter and canister filters. "Squeaky clean" is the name of the game here, and gravel provides a place for detritus and non-beneficial bacteria to repose. Another option here is to utilize living sand and live rocks. This refers to sand that is taken from the ocean (or cultivated in an ocean system) and to rocks that have also been taken

from the ocean and are colonized by numerous animals, as well as coralline algae. The point is that living sand contains many microorganisms, as well as detritus-eating tiny sea cucumbers, crabs, and starfish, so the sand doesn't need an undergravel filter. In this case, though, the fishes must really be selected with care, as many species will eat all of those beneficial invertebrates, plucking them right out of the sand!

Most definitely, a protein skimmer is called for in a tank containing a minireef, although I have seen a few that seemed to thrive with only trickle filtration. The point

The type of high-intensity lighting required to allow photosynthetic algae living symbiotically with *Tridacna* clams and other invertebrates also provides illumination required by free-swimming algae that might have to be removed from the tank through filtration. Photo by U. Erich Friese.

The keeping of both hard corals (a *Lobophyllia* species, probably *L. hemprichii,* shown above) and soft corals (a species of the soft coral genus *Xenia* shown below, with large *Discosoma* disc anemones visible at right) was once viewed as almost impossible of achievement by an aquarist who didn't have continuing access to a supply of clean ocean water, but the progress that has been made in gaining knowledge of marine animals' requirements, coupled with the great increase in effectiveness of aquarium equipment, has made their keeping much easier. Photos by U. Erich Friese.

Living rocks form the basis for filtration arrangements set up along the lines of "natural" filtration methods and are the backbone of many minireef setups. These living rocks have a coating of algae. Photo by U. Erich Friese.

is that the more redundancy that you have, the better chance you have of success. The minireef tank is a splendid example of aquarium accomplishment, but it takes a special type of person to have success with this type of tank. The hobbyist should be virtually obsessed by life in the sea and should actually enjoy doing little chores to maintain the tank. Don't let anyone kid you. A minireef tank can be quite demanding of your time. But most minireef hobbyists don't mind.

COMMENTS

Most hobbyists develop an affinity for a particular type of filtration system. That very fact argues for the idea that no one filtration system has been proven a clear winner over all of the others. I tend to favor simplicity. I'll use reverse-flow undergravel filtration whenever possible. But, alas, since I have been smitten by cichlids, I must often substitute with the canister filter. In a similar way, I have a fondness for marine animals, so I have used wet/dry filtration, too. Although I have a certain direction, I can't absolutely recommend one filtration system over another. Besides, who knows what exciting new developments the future will bring!

THE NATURAL AQUARIUM

It is generally taken for granted that we all try to make our aquaria as "natural" as possible. The emphasis in this case here is to replace gadgets and have biological filtration take place through the inhabitants of the aquarium. This can be plants in the case of freshwater aquaria or animals in the case of marine aquaria. Of course, those "true rulers, " the bacteria, will have a hand in each one. The fact is that a primary compromise that must be made in the case of natural tanks, both freshwater and marine, is that the fishes must be given a lower priority than they normally have. In the case of the freshwater tank, the plants have priority; with the marine tank, it is the invertebrates that have top billing. Also, a low fish population must be maintained in order for even the best of these natural systems to work. Let us begin first with the freshwater types.

THE LEIDEN AQUARIUM

The natural aquarium in the freshwater world consists primarily of plants, and it is named after a Dutch city in which that system of aquaculture was pioneered. Perhaps I should say that it was rediscovered there. In the early days, there were not many good air pumps or good filters, so everyone who kept aquaria—and there weren't very many of us in those days—tended to try to keep a "balanced" aquarium. That is, the idea was to have a natural

Facing page and above: Freshwater aquaria that contain many plants and either no fishes at all or just a few small ones need much less filtration than aquaria with a normal (by aquarium hobby standards) fish population. Photo above by M.-P. and C. Piednoir, Aqua Press; facing page photo by van Raam.

To create an aquarium scene as attractive as this usually means that the needs of the plants have to be to some extent sacrificed to the needs of the fishes, and filtration is geared to the needs of the fishes almost exclusively. Photo by M.-P. and C. Pienoir, Aqua Press.

nitrogen cycle. Also, the plants would supply the oxygen, and the animals would supply the nitrate for the plants.

In theory, this sounds great, but in practice it is quite difficult to attain. It may be a natural process in nature, but in the aquarium the fish population is usually too high for there to be a natural nitrogen cycle. The plants simply become overwhelmed by the amount of nitrate. Of course, it is possible to do partial water changes to compensate and allow the plants a chance to catch up, but the early aquarists were not inclined to make partial water changes. Remember, they had the idea that there was something magical about old water.

The general philosophy behind the Leiden aquarium is to emphasize the plants, to keep a low population of generally small fishes, and to maintain the tank without filtration or even aeration. The only artificial things are the heater and the intense lighting for the plants. Hence there is no bubbling of filters or airstones. The tank is quiet and placid.

The usual approach is to start the tank out with plants first. Since plants grow best in fine sand, that is what is used, and no undergravel filter is installed. There can even be a little plant food mixed with the sand, as you won't have fishes in the tank for a while anyway. Once the plants are all growing well, the fish are introduced, but this may be months after the tank was set up. Only a few are kept at first, to make sure that the tank is properly "cycled"; that is, that the nitrifying bacteria have become established in the tank. The beauty of this system is that the plants will take up the nitrate and make use of the nitrogen contained within the compound. Theoretically,

Exposure to sunlight causes the water in many outdoor ponds to turn green with algae, and although it is possible to remove a portion of the algal population through mechanical filtration, ultra–violet sterilizers are much more effective. Photo by M.-P. and C. Piednoir, Aqua Press.

Only a very small fish population can be maintained in a freshwater aquarium in which plants are intended to function as the main processors of the nitrogenous compounds produced by the fishes. Photo by Doshin Kobayashi.

water changes should not have to be frequent. But, remember, the fishes are swimming in their own waste, and it is unlikely that the plants will be able to keep up with it unless you have a tiny population of tiny fishes. For that reason, it is best to make regular partial water changes. A ten percent change on a weekly basis will easily suffice if your tank is not over-stocked.

Oxygen is supplied by the plants for the fish, but it should be kept in mind that the plants' production of oxygen stops in darkness—and that is one reason that a large fish population cannot be kept.

In general, the Leiden tank is going to appeal to those who really like plants and are not that crazy about gadgets. Part of its beauty is its simplicity. The disadvantage of the system is that the fish population must be kept low, and many fascinating species must be excluded. However, a beautifully planted tank can be absolutely spectacular.

THE NATURAL MARINE SYSTEM

Eng's System (The Original Natural System)

Just for the information of the reader, not many people utilize this completely natural approach in the same way as Lee Chin Eng did back in the early 1960s, as there is always something that most reef hobbyists feel can be improved. Besides that, we don't (at least, most of us don't) have access to a tropical sun the way Lee Chin Eng did in Indonesia. If you have an air conditioned room and don't have to worry about overheating the water, you could place your tank to take advantage of what natural sunlight there is and supplement it with the high-intensity, wide-spectrum fluorescent lighting that has been designed for reef tanks. The point is, though, that you don't need to rely on natural sunlight, except as a tribute to Mr. Eng.

Lee Chin Eng of Djakarta, Indonesia with a marine aquarium set up according to his "natural system" precepts, for which he became well known in the early 1960s.

One of the reasons there were so many failures when aquarists attempted to copy Eng's system was that hobbyists failed to realize the patience that was needed to get seeded live rock and live sand fully functioning before adding some of the other animals. Also, receiving shipped live rocks is not like taking them from the ocean and placing them into your tank the same day, even within the hour, as Eng was able to do.

A decision is needed at this point. Live rock and live sand can be expensive. However, if you have a hundred-gallon aquarium (for example), you can simply fill the bottom of the tank with coral sand. Then you can order only minute amounts of live sand, and it will eventually serve to "seed" your coral gravel with the microorganisms and the tiny crustaceans that will make your living sand functional. But it will take about six months for this to happen.

The same is true of live rock. You can simply decorate the tank with calcareous rock and, again, it will become seeded with the different types of bacteria that are needed. That way, you can order a smaller amount of actual live rock. If you decide to do things in this way, they will be simpler, but there is much patience needed to wait for six months. Maybe that's a good thing, because patience is the most important virtue of the natural reef aquarist.

If you decide to use a basic stock of inert sand and rock, set your tank up with the basic sand and rock first.

Place about two inches of sand in the tank; you'll need plenty of rockwork, as it will be functioning as one of your main filters. Use either synthetic ocean water or (much less likely) natural sea water. The point here is that a little natural ocean water will help seed your tank with the proper bacteria and possibly even beneficial plankton. At this point, you don't have to worry about disease coming in to infect any of your animals. Let the tank sit for a few days and check the water parameters to make sure that everything is okay. Nothing should go wrong; after all, you have hardly anything living in the tank at this point. Place airstones in strategic locations. That is, place them beneath the rock so that currents are created. It is also a good idea to place some bags of high-quality activated carbon near the airstones. This is a modification of Eng's system, but dissolved organic compounds can eventually turn the water yellow. Activated carbon will help prevent this. And placing the bags near an airstone will help ensure that all of the water is filtered through them.

One of the features of Eng's system was to have some air hoses without

For the first week, you may want to keep the lighting turned off so that algal growth doesn't become rampant. You will get a certain amount of die-off of microorganisms even with the best live rock, and the dead organic matter will lead to a build-up of phosphates that can really drive a bloom of algae. After a couple of weeks, you can turn on your lighting, and it would be a good idea at this time to introduce a few turbo snails. These are herbivorous snails,

coral and other invertebrates doing well for at least six months, you can think about adding some fish to the tank.

THE PLENUM TANK

Now let's go to the plenum tank, the one with the emphasis on live sand and a space of water at the bottom. There is an upper sand level, a screen, and then a lower sand level that is anoxic. Superficially, the construction looks something like an undergravel filter. There is a deep bed of

A very heavy growth of algae in a marine aquarium. Photo by Dr. D. Terver.

airstones underneath at least one concave rock. That way large volumes of air would build up under the rock(s) and then bubble to the surface, creating some turbulence and wave action, which is believed to be beneficial for the corals and anemones. At this point, you can send for the live rocks and living sand.

and they will help control the growth of algae.

After six months, check your water parameters (although presumably you have been doing this all along and entering the results in your log book). If everything is okay—and it should be—you can think about which corals to add. After you have the

sand, but there is no attempt to circulate the water through it. In fact, the filter is sometimes called an anoxic filter because it is totally deprived of oxygen, and that happens in the sand layers. That is exactly the opposite of what is intended with the undergravel filter. In the sand above the plenum, various biological processes are at work day and night to improve the quality of the water. Some of these processes reduce nitrate to a harmless gas, some liberate calcium, some boost alkalinity, and others ensure that dangerous products like hydrogen sulfide will not become a problem.

This type of filter was originally the brainchild of Dr. Jean Jaubert at the University of Nicc in France, and it was introduced in the 1980s. Starting from the bottom, it involves some type of lifts for holding the filter plate. The filter is popular enough that special plates with the lifts included are being manufactured. However, it is possible to use egg crating diffusers for fluorescent lighting or PVC piping as lifts. An important point is that a tank of up to 100 gallons in capacity should have a plenum (space) of about one inch. In aquaria of between 100 and 500 gallons, it is recommended the plenum be one to three inches in height. Whatever you use for supporting the filter plate, remember that live rock will be added later on, so their added weight should be kept in mind. At this point I should mention that this type of tank has become sufficiently popular that some acrylic tanks are sold specifically for use as such, and they are complete with the necessary plenum and screening mechanisms for the bottom, not to mention custom lighting hoods and stands.

After the plenum area is installed, it is time for the first layer of sand. The hobbyists who have been having the best success with this system have been using aragonite sand. Again, the economical route to take here is to get lots of base sand and simply seed it with living sand. In fact, I don't know of anyone who doesn't proceed in that way. Since the sand you have may be small enough to fall through the filter plate, it is a good idea to have fiberglass screening cover the plate. Then place at least an inch of sand on top of that layer; two inches would be better. Place screening over that layer and add four more inches of sand.

One reason so many people start with inert sand is that then you don't get the nutrient enrichment that will cause algal growths or other problems. Aragonite sand is more soluble than calcite and most other types of sands. The drawback to starting out in this way is that it will require more patience on the

A representation of Dr. Jaubert's "natural" system, with the plenum area and anoxic zone at the bottom of the tank. Drawing by John Quinn.

part of the hobbyist to bring the system up to its full bioload carrying capacity than if all live sand were used. Also, there appear to be some trace amounts of silicate present in aragonite, which can initially cause a brown diatom algae condition. This is easily controlled, either by eliminating light during startup or, if you turn the lights on right from the beginning of the startup period, by vacuuming the upper surface of the substrate as required.

rock. As guidance for your decision, there is the following to consider. Eventually, your sand will become live; that is, it will be colonized by the desirable microorganisms. However, living sand is not overly expensive, and you don't have to get a lot of it for simple seeding purposes, so you will be able to make a minimum order. Additionally, many hobbyists are convinced that some of the organisms that live in the sand are not likely to be found in even the best of live rocks.

with live rock, there is a certain amount of initial die-off of some of the organisms, making the organic content associated with the newly received sand very high. Not only may the organic level be high, it may also be coated with orthophosphate. If placed directly in the aquarium, it could lead to algae problems in the start-up cycle. For that reason, in order to lessen its organic content, live sand should receive a gentle flushing with some freshly made seawater

A minireef tank housing a very sparse fish population but a wide array of invertebrates in a sparklingly clear environment. Photo by Mark Smith.

At this point there is, once again, a choice. You can send for some live sand and allow a few months for the sand to become fully colonized by bacteria, various worms, and crustaceans. Or you can place live rock into the tank immediately and wait for the sand to be colonized by the very same organisms from the live

Remember that live sand is called "live" simply because it contains various types of living bacteria and various invertebrates, such as brittle stars, sea cucumbers, and crustaceans, which keep the sand clear of detritus and keep it turned, much as earthworms do in good-quality soil. As is the case

before going into your aquarium. This is especially important if you are filling your aquarium with live sand rather than doing it the cheaper but patience-requiring way.

With the plenum system, most hobbyists prefer to use at least fifty percent base rock. If you do it that way, the

Placement of rockwork and corals within a tank so as to allow water to circulate freely is desirable, since it imitates natural reef conditions. Photo by Bob Goemans.

rock can be placed into the tank at this time (about thirty days after the live sand is placed). Another option is to place the base rock into the tank immediately after placing in the live sand, but concentrate all of your attention on the sand. Think of it as your primary filter. For that reason, you want to make sure that you arrange your rock in such a way that currents of water can get to the sand. For example, large rocks can be propped up by smaller ones, in order to ensure water movement over the sand. Many hobbyists place the rock on PVC piping or some other such support so that the sand is not covered by the rock. Passages for currents are quite common on the coral reef, and the natural reef systems seem to function better if they are provided.

Not only do you want to provide props of some kind to keep the rockwork up off the sand and allow circulation under the rocks, but you also want to arrange the rocks in such a way that water will circulate well between them. The more spaces between the rocks the better, but remember that the rocks will eventually be called upon to hold up the other live rocks and eventually the various types of corals and anemones. The point is that it is important to set the rocks up so that there are as many spaces as possible between them, but they should still be stable enough to support their own weight easily and to eventually support the weight of corals and clams. And remember that both corals and clams are going to grow and become heavier.

Leave the lights off for the next thirty days. Use a turkey baster or a vacuum to remove any matter that falls off the rocks onto the sand. Any obvious die-off of some type on the rocks should be vacuumed off, too.

After about thirty days, you can add the live rock. The rock should be rinsed with freshly mixed sea water, just as the live sand was, and for the same reason. You want to get rid of as much dead organic matter as possible. Leave the lights off for another thirty-day period and keep the rock clean. The idea still is to keep the organic level very low. In fact, one variation here is to utilize an inside protein skimmer or one of those small combination trickle filters with a protein skimmer in the filter. This is an option but certainly not essential, as eventually the protein skimmer would have to be shut down anyway. The idea under this system is not to have artificial filters competing with the biological filters that will

Corals (*Montastraea cavernosa)* and heavily encrusted living rock form the basis of this starkly beautiful underwater scene—one that is coming to be replicated more and more often in home aquaria through the use of modern aquarium filtration equipment. Photo by Rafael Mesa.

develop. The only reason for using a protein skimmer in the beginning is that we just don't want to overwhelm the natural filters before they are colonized by all the various bacteria. That is why we are so careful about organic matter at this time.

When the second thirty-day period has expired and everything looks clean and settled in and your water parameters are good, it is time to turn on the lights and add the corals and other invertebrates. It is half their carrying capacity. There is nothing like allowing things to happen *slowly* to ensure complete success. Again, turbo snails are a real friend to have at this point to keep back the growth of algae.

After you have most of your corals established and doing well, you can add the fishes that you intend to use. Real sticklers don't add any fishes at all until they have their entire complement of corals, clams, and anemones. Fishes have been known to treat lately. There are exciting new things being learned in each area. I would be remiss, however, if I did not emphasize that we have been given the advantage of some great filtration breakthroughs over the years. The drawback to all the natural systems is that the fish population must be severely limited. Most of us are in the hobby mainly for the fishes. For that reason, most of us are going to want to make use of an artificial filtration system. The only problem is

A view into an irregularly but attractively shaped minireef aquarium set up on the sales floor of a tropical fish shop. Model aquaria like this one do a good job of popularizing the aquarium hobby. Photo by Jason Prime.

best to add these a few at a time. In fact, if you have the patience, add just one a week. That way you can make sure that the new animal is doing well and it doesn't overwhelm your natural filters (i.e. the live sand, plenum, and rocks) with too much bioload for them to handle. At this stage of the game, your biological filters will be at only about newly introduced corals as possible food, and that should not be surprising, since the fishes are used to anything that is put into the tank as being food.

Closing Comments

I wanted to include the natural tanks, both freshwater and of the marine type, as they have created a lot of attention choosing the system, and even that is not a big problem. All the systems have their good points, and that is why they all have adherents. I have told you something about the different systems and told you about the ones that I particularly like. It is now your choice. Have fun and enjoy the adventure of aquarium keeping.

GLOSSARY

I am including a glossary for those who aren't used to some of the marine terms used in this book and also as a reference for some terms that may have a general applicability in matters related to aquarium filtration.

Actinic lighting: The ultraviolet part of the sun's rays that produce chemical changes, such as in photosynthesis or photography—or sunburns!

Aerobic: In the presence of oxygen. Aerobic bactcria thrive in oxygen's presence. Anaerobic (without oxygen) live best without oxygen molecules, but they still need oxygen, which they take in the form of atoms from nitrate, thus breaking it down.

Airstones: Devices for producing a multitude of bubbles in the aquarium. Airstones once were nearly always made of pumice rock; hence the name "air*stones.*" But they are often made of plastic or wood these days and are improved in function.

Anaerobic: See "aerobic."

Anemones: Sea anemones are named after the flower because of their resemblance to it. They are, of course, animals, and they could accurately be described as upside-down jellyfish, with the stinging tentacles sticking upward. Even the giant tropical anemones in which clownfishes reside don't hurt most people's hands to the touch, but some people experience a stinging sensation and even a rash. Anemo-nes can, of course, be lethal to fishes and other marine creatures. They can harm corals as well.

Aragonite: A mineral that occurs as rock or sand and has a high percentage of calcium carbonate and strontium carbonate.

Atoll: A reef that forms around an oceanic island. Usually the island was volcanic and eventually sank (as hypothesized by Charles Darwin and later confirmed by scientists). This leaves a string of coral reefs encircling a lagoon.

Autotroph: An organism that is able to synthesize food from inorganic materials; plants and bacteria are autotrophic. Normally, the process is photosynthesis, but anaerobic bacteria are able to utilize combinations of atoms for the purpose (as are some other bacteria).

Base rocks: Calacareous rocks that form the base of a reef aquarium. They are eventually colonized by marine organisms, including bacteria, to the point that they themselves become "living rocks."

Blue-green algae: Also known as cyanobacteria, these bacteria form an undesirable slime in the aquarium, but they can be controlled by maintaining low phosphate levels and keeping detritus siphoned out of the aquarium.

Calcification: The process by which corals and coralline algae extract calcium from the water and deposit it as en-crusting calcium carbonate.

Calcium: A major element involved in the building of calcareous organisms, such as stony corals.

Chemical filter: A filter that removes solids and gases by chemical means. This usually refers to activated carbon, but it can also refer to nitrate and phosphate removers.

Compound filter: A combination of different filters and devices, including biological filters, protein skimmers, and denitrator devices.

Coralline algae: Red, purple, and pink encrusting algae that envelop rocks and form calcareous crusts like coral.

Fluidized bed filtration: The ultimate evolution of the undergravel filter, this filter keeps sand in suspension, thus ensuring the exposure of each grain to the water and its nutrients and oxygen. A very effective biological filter.

Filter feeders: Organisms that feed upon other organisms or materials held in suspension in the water. Corals and tube worms are examples of such feeders.

Fringing reef: A reef that develops along the coastline of an island or continent.

Hard corals: These include the reef-building corals, but some of the hard corals kept by hobbyists are solitary and don't build reefs.

Kalkwasser: This is German for lime water, but American manufacturers have made products that include it and are recommended to be included in top-off water (to replace evaporated water) or to be added with trace elements.

Living rock: Rock that has been in the ocean and contains microorganisms, encrusting coralline algae, worms, and other marine organisms. Since many modern live rocks were cultivated in the aquarium, the first part of this definition may eventually be modified.

Living sand: This is similar to live rock. It is sand that has been in the ocean (or cultivated in an aquarium) that contains marine bacteria and invertebrates that help maintain the quality of the water in the tank.

Log: A daily (or almost daily!) record that is kept of observations made of the reef tank and of measurements of its physical and chemical parameters. At first the keeping of a log seems silly, but its value is soon apparent.

Mineral: An inorganic substance other than water.

Nitrogen cycle: This refers to the nitrogen-containing wastes being converted from ammonia to nitrite to nitrate and to the eventual release of the nitrogen (if we have anaerobic bacteria, algae, or plants).

Ozonizer: Either a reactor or ultraviolet light that produces ozone, a highly reactive form of oxygen that tends to break down organic compounds.

Powerheads: Pumps that were originally designed to pump water forcefully up from undergravel filters. They are useful in reef tanks for provid-

ing currents that are beneficial to corals and other organisms.

Protein skimmer: This is a device that has proved especially useful in reef tanks. It strips organic matter from the water. There are many types, but they all need daily attention as to the bubble flow and emptying of the foam cups.

Redox potential: Basically, a measurement of the water's purity (that is, its freedom from organic contaminants). It is measured electrically and expressed in millivolts, with higher readings indicating cleaner water.

Soft corals: Soft corals may be soft or leathery, and some even produce a stony sort of skeleton, but they are not of the reef-building type, as are many of the hard corals.

Specific gravity: The measure of the weight of a given material to that of pure water. Distilled water has a specific gravity of 1.00, while sea water ranges from 1.020 to 1.030. We can infer salinity from specific gravity.

Sump: The reservoir below the dry part of a trickle filter or in a filter or reservoir behind the tank.

Trace elements: Elements, such as barium, lithium, iron, and molybdenum, that naturally occur in sea water and have been found to be of benefit to marine organisms and are therefore added to synthetic sea water.

Trickle filtration: This filtration is also called wet-dry filtration and is an attempt to give the bacteria as much exposure to air as possible. While such devices have their

faults, they have been a big step toward keeping living corals.

Tridacnid clams: Clams that are often kept in reef tanks, as they have zooxanthellae in their mantles, enabling them to prosper even without being fed (although they are filter feeders). Some of these clams, such as *Tridacna gigas*, are the ones pictured in the popular press as capturing divers by the foot. Although such a portrayal is erroneous, some species do become huge, soon outgrowing the home aquarium.

Ultraviolet light: High-energy shortwave light that can be harmful to organisms but also provides the energy for photosynthesis.

Ultraviolet sterilizer: A device that radiates the water with ultraviolet rays. Since such rays are harmful to organisms, the devices are shielded, and the water is pumped though them.

Undergravel filtration: The original successful filters for marine aquaria, undergravel filters function by causing oxygenated water to flow through a bed of gravel or similarly sized inorganic material placed directly above them. Usually made in the form of flat plates, these filters are not used with reef tanks except in extremely rare instances.

Zooxanthellae: Microscopic flagellates that live symbiotically in the tissues of corals, anemones, and tridacnid clams, producing food for themselves and their hosts through photosynthesis, just like plants.